Empowerment in Organizations

Empowerment in Organizations

The Theory and Practice of a Mandate System

by
Cornelis Pieterse

Rudolf Steiner College Press

ISBN 0-945803-87-7

Rudolf Steiner College Press
9200 Fair Oaks Blvd.
Fair Oaks, CA 95628, U.S.A.

This book is dedicated to my parents
Jeanne Adriane van Goch and Cor Pieterse
and to my wife
Mickey
for their love and selfless support.

Contents

Foreword

This publication represents insights and practices developed over 18 years as a consultant and facilitator in the business and non-profit sectors, especially Waldorf schools. It is my hope that it serves as a practical guide for individuals and groups working in all aspects of organizational life including collegial relationships. Much of what is written is also relevant to more informal relationships.

There are two basic themes running through this book. One is the theory and practice of a mandate system. But no mandate system can be designed or executed without the requisite skill set in communication, decision making, conflict resolution, meeting effectiveness, and facilitation. These required skills are an integral part of what it means to work with mandates. Additionally, an overview is given on developmental phases in organizations. Such understanding will greatly assist in gaining a deeper appreciation of the universal laws underlying all human and organization development, as the two are closely intertwined.

These insights affect how we view the world, and *how we view the world determines how we act in it*. From this we may gain inspiration at those times when the minutia of daily life threaten to dampen commitment and enthusiasm for our respective fields of endeavor.

The second theme is closely related to the first theme in that a mandate system presupposes a decentralized governing structure. Such a structure changes the roles and responsibilities of leaders and followers into a different paradigm. This new paradigm places especially stringent obligations on followers that one would not usually demand from grass-roots and front line members. Traditional roles become less relevant to the reality of running effective organizations. Organizational charts and hierarchical power structures hardly ever reflected the reality one would find in organizations anyway. Now they diminish in importance altogether, gradually being replaced by an institutional awareness of the ever-changing conditions and requirements of the moment. Few of us find comfort in this uncertainty (especially when it comes to organizational life), but the distress of struggling with intractable problems on all levels of society is even greater.

People are searching for creative and lasting solutions—searching for community in the workplace and neighborhoods, searching for collaborative enterprises, searching for meaning and purpose in their lives and work, searching for colleagues and for partners, searching for empowerment from the grass-root level up. In the words of Peter Block, a pioneer on leadership questions:

> The age of the leader has come and gone. Our fixation with the leader has us celebrate the heroism of the individual at the expense of communal successes. If we just let leadership be, and choose to focus on citizenship, we affirm democracy and create accountable, high-performing institutions.

In the Waldorf movement at least, much has been spoken about the mandate system. Yet, a lot of confusion, misunderstanding, and even skepticism about its value persist. I hope this book can assist in making mandates a realistic and empowering method for managing our complex institutions. When the mandate system is fully integrated in the running of an organization, it can become its lifeblood.

Realizing how much my philosophical, theoretical and culturally determined lenses color even the simplest of observations and recommendations, I thought it necessary to include these perspectives in this text. Doing so may position readers best to examine and compare their perspectives with mine. Scattered throughout are various observations and reflections on social and organizational life I gained over many years of consulting. Additionally, I thought it important to turn a somewhat critical eye at the culture of ideology-based institutions. For all the spiritual wealth and material health these institutions bring to the world, their work culture may cast a shadow—as all cultures do—which can sabotage or even destroy from within the power to do the good. Margaret Wheatley has observed that:

> We create organizations from the outside, imposing these limiting designs on the rich desires of those who have come together. Over time, the organization that was created in response to some deep call becomes a rigid structure that impedes fulfilling that call. People come to resent the organization they created, because now it is a major impediment to their creativity, to their faith, to their purposeful dreams.

In fact, the closer we get to our "purposeful dreams," the stronger our individual and collective weaknesses will assert themselves in opposition. *Like a finely attuned sixth sense, the world will zero-in on what we have not wanted to see ourselves, and confront us with our shortcomings.* The only antidote to this ever-present danger is for us to acknowledge our shadows and bring them to light whereby they may lose their counterproductive influence.

Where appropriate, I have italicized principles by which processes can be designed to reach desired results. It is truly in these principles where reality and theory meet, irrespective of our colored lenses or theoretical preferences. *Principles are like the points on a compass. They are not reality itself but provide a tool for orientation through a maze of competing "real" facts and solutions.* If readers at least familiarize themselves with these principles, they may learn to distinguish between what is universal and what is unique in their situation. To the extent that a particular situation and organization is unique, it will require a calibrated approach by which to find effective and creative ways of working.

If one assumes, as I do, that our inner development and enlightenment can no longer be obtained outside the social and organizational (work) context in which we find ourselves, then the methodologies described in this book are as much a guide to effective management as they are individual and collective tools in our search for truth and meaning in a mode of continuous learning. This book will have achieved its goal when in the practice of these methodologies the mundane and the profound are no longer distinguishable.

Acknowledgment

For most of my adult life, I have immersed myself in anthroposophy (Rudolf Steiner (1861–1925). This philosophy provides me with a comprehensive worldview by which to explore the worlds within and outside myself (Wachsmuth 1955). Almost all of my perspectives on life—even life itself—I owe to this "science of the spirit." I have found that in anthroposophy the immensely practical and the deeply esoteric become one.

This book could never have been written were it not for the encouragement, gentle reminders, guilt trips, wisdom, editing support, and above all friendship of each of the following people plus many others with whom I shared significant conversations and life-affirming tasks.

I owe everything to my soul partner and wife, Mickey, because of her unwavering support and faith in me so many years before I began to have faith in myself. I would like to thank the late Francis Edmunds from Emerson College, UK, who gave me inspiration and a new world of opportunity, and my soul brother Rube Cubale from The Mid-Atlantic Association of Trainers and Consultants, whose deep humanity and incredible facilitation skills gave me a living example how I too can become an artist of life. I am indebted to the faculty and fellow students of the Psychology Department of Antioch New England Graduate School in New Hampshire, who helped me love and accept human beings in all their dimensions, and to Christopher Schaefer (Envision Associates), and Ned Hulbert (Growing Edge Partners, Inc.) who introduced me to the consulting profession. Thanks also go to Claude Julien from the Rudolf Steiner College Press for offering the opportunity to publish this book and to all those who generously agreed to review the manuscript.

Kind permission was granted by David Mitchell, publications chair of AWSNA, to extensively rework and adapt my previously published articles on The Mandate System, Communication Guidelines and Working with Conflict. (Chapters 6, 7 and 11.) Dino Biris from Semasea Organization Development, and Ned Hulbert et al. from Growing Edge Partners, Inc., kindly granted me permission to work with their model of the Three Decision-making Modes in Chapter 9.

And finally, but not least, love to my life-long friends and co-creators of a magical stage called the Lemnis Conference Series in the Pacific Northwest on which we played so many times: Anne Davidson, Valerie Hope, Kathy Fraser, Donna Nett, Martin Novom and Herb Walsh.

Part One

Conceptual Framework

1

Systems Thinking

I use the word *system* to mean an entity that has many interacting and interdependent parts and components that together form a whole. While the concept of systems often refers to more mechanical processes, it also applies to all living organisms. Social life, too, must be considered a system or organism. The family is a system, as are groups, organizations and entire nations. There also are systems within systems. Sets of interactive elements simultaneously influence each other to form and maintain an organism or system (Yalom 1985 and Napier 1988). Ecosystems are wonderful examples of this principle, as are complex biological organisms like the human body. We know that all organisms and species, together with the forces of nature, are totally dependent on each other for their well-being and continued existence. The entire system slowly evolves while maintaining a delicate equilibrium among its individual parts.

We could speak of a "social ecology" when we refer to people gathering in groups or working in companies, or the collective of all peoples on the earth. Martin Luther King, Jr. expressed this principle beautifully:

> All men are caught in an inescapable network of mutuality, tied in a single garment of destiny. Whatever affects one directly, affects all indirectly.

The most basic tenet in systems theory is that the whole is greater than the sum total of its parts. Again, this is true in biological as well as in social systems. In anthroposophical literature, it is suggested that specific spiritual beings unite with humans as soon as two or more of us are gathered together. All of us can independently verify this truth when observing groups and organizations. *Each organization has a unique personality all of its own—with a culture clearly discernable but not always easily put into words and moving through evolutionary stages of development.*

Another tenet in systems theory is that cause and effect is circular in nature rather than linear. The parts (human beings) of a system (organization) are unique but mutually related. Like a mobile hanging from the ceiling, when you disturb one part the rest immediately responds and adjusts, which in turn affects the movement and placement of the original part. Gradually the system comes to a relative rest (homeostasis) until the next intervention.

Unlike the case of the mobile, in human relationships the cords and bars are invisible and may date back to prenatal conditions asserting their influence on us today. And also unlike the situation of the mobile, the intervention or disturbance can come both from without or within the system. Even a truly free initiative—one not compelled by outer circumstances or by force of habit—can only take place within the social context in which it was initiated. In other words, a free deed never stands in isolation from all the circumstances surrounding it.

We are imbedded in a "network of mutuality." This fact has huge ramifications when we consider how we work in our organizations and collegial relationships. If we continue to persist in a type of thinking that can blame one person as "the problem" in a conflict, or persist in thinking that external negative economic conditions have nothing to with how we work and think inside the business world, viable and lasting solutions will never be found. Instead, the solutions of yesterday will only become the problems of today. World events since September 2001 illustrate this principle powerfully. Those of us working in anthroposophical and Waldorf-related communities are no less vulnerable to this faulty way of thinking. With all inquiries into the nature of social life, we first have to completely re-school our deeply ingrained linear-based thinking with thinking capable of comprehending the multidirectional causality of all human interactions. We can call this type of living thinking *heart-based*.

It is a thinking that can hold two opposing views at the same time. It is a thinking that can see pattern and themes, instead of just individual isolated facts. It is a type of thinking that can assimilate and appreciate esthetic qualities without losing the clarity of logic.

2

The Context in which We Find Ourselves

Our world seems to be changing in dramatic ways. I am sure that every generation since the beginning of modern civilization has made that assertion. But the technological advances of today seem to race ahead of what any single human being can comprehend, no matter how well schooled in various disciplines. These technological advances are matched, if not surpassed, by the subtle changes in consciousness. The perceptions we generally hold of the world and of ourselves are irreversibly changed once we see our blue globe suspended in outer space. I could imagine that previously only gods were privileged to this sight. *To watch our earth from thousands of miles away, we have come to be aware of the fragility, the interconnectedness and absolute interdependence of all living creatures on this planet.* These concepts of interconnectedness and interdependence have become our reality rather than just interesting ideas.

An article in *Life* magazine (Rosenfeld 1965) traced the development of an embryo from just after conception to birth. Like the image from outer space, these images have a powerful and lasting effect on how we think about things. Miraculously, a single cell forms and then replicates itself in its likeness. These two cells repeat the process exponentially until an undifferentiated and unspecialized mass of cells exits. These cells at that moment represent pure potentiality. Then the equally miraculous process of differentiation takes place at the expense of limitless potentiality. Cells irreversibly commit to forming specific organs with specific functions.

At what point in the development of a young business or service organization do we see pure potential before it turns into differentiated functions and specialties? *Could it be that an idea to manufacture a product, or the vision to serve a particular mission is equal to the unlimited potential of cells before it is manifested into reality?*

On the very edge of scientific thinking and exploration, scientists are confronted with a phenomenon that seems not to answer natural laws. Under certain conditions, subatomic particles may appear as wave or as particle, codetermined as it is by the perspective of the observer (Briggs 1971). Astronomy is now talking of black holes, negative space, imploding galaxies, and anti-matter to describe what is being observed. In fact, observation and theory seem to play leapfrog over each other. Each theory becomes a gateway to new observations, and each observation compels a re-examination of long-held assumptions, including the erroneous notion that the observer has no influence on what is observed. The very nature of these theories and concepts gives an indication that we are venturing beyond the study of matter into those formative forces that seem to order matter and the psyche (Laszlo 1993 and Conforti 1999). Scientists now are talking about Field Theory (Loye 1983), Synchronicity and Complexity Theory (Lewin 1992), Chaos (Gleick 1987) and the Principle of Self-Organization and String Theory. Instead of pursuing a search ad infinitum for the smallest and most irreducible building blocks to explain the nature of matter, these scientific inquiries focus on a total set of phenomena. They are discovering fields of energy and patterns of development that apply across disparate organisms (Casto 2000). This new way of looking at creation permeates many academic and artistic disciplines.

It is no accident, in my view, that the cusp of scientific exploration simultaneously unfolds in the direction of the farthest regions of the universe and the world of microbiology and particle physics. These two opposite directions of inquiry seem to meet at their extreme ends only to discover they share similar laws and principles.

To see the universe in a grain of sand.
—William Blake

It makes sense that principles underlying the formation of solar systems and galaxies also apply to subatomic structures.

In our management and organizational problem solving practices, are we keeping pace with the daring explorations of other disciplines, or are we still content to replicate models whose roots reach into the autocratic and hierarchical institutions of the past? These autocratic institutions are still found in every form of human endeavor and experience today. If our world, in all its human aspects, were safer and healthier, more equitable and more beneficial to all, we could make a powerful argument for these outdated models. But the near chaotic conditions of the present dictate a serious reexamination of our assumptions and ways of working.

This reexamination must encompass how we think of and exercise leadership (DePree 1992). What are the appropriate organizational structures and decision-making modes? Who has access to what kind of information? How do we interface with the rest of the world, especially those who have differing philosophies and cultures? Who can speak to the spiritual identity of an organization? Some of these questions will be addressed in the next chapters.

3

Phases in Organizational Development

What is development anyway?

It is important for us to come to a deeper understanding of the nature of development, because all biological and social systems follow a path of development. The literal meaning of the concept of development is: the opposite of envelopment. Development points to the essence of an organism or living being by unwrapping the obstructing layers as it passes through the evolution of birth, maturation, decline, death, and rebirth.

Usually when people talk about development in their organizations, they really mean unlimited growth to become something ever bigger and better. But it is unrealistic to expect unlimited growth in a business or institution (yet that's all we do and plan for), as much as it is unrealistic to expect that our bodies will live forever. It is not that we should plan for our businesses and institutions to fail at some time in the future. *However, once an organization is well established, we can begin to aim for missions that reach beyond the original mission by providing additional services and products for other than our traditional constituencies.*

Development unfolds in phases, each phase having its own characteristics and time frame. Organizational principles and laws apply to all forms of life in nature and the evolution of the earth, as well as to human cultures. As the force of gravity pervades all matter, so do these principles pervade all developing organisms.

Stages of development follow each other in more or less predictable order. In the case of human beings—after the bodily nature has reached full maturation and begins to follow a path of gradual decline in strength, flexibility and renewal—their further development pertains to the soul, mind, and spirit. Maturation and active learning of new skills and insights becomes a matter of inner discipline and determination. It is in the last phases of human development that glimpses of the innermost core of the human spirit can be manifested. The same holds for the later phases in a developing organization.

Some Principles of Development

Professor Bernard Lievegoed (1902–1996) from the Netherlands Pedagogical Institute was one of the first scholars to distinguish phases of development in organizations, no matter the type of organization. So too, he describes the intellectual and psychological phases of development in human beings (Lievegoed 1973, 1979). Professor Lievegoed identified three distinct phases: (1) the Pioneer or Initiative Phase, (2) the Differentiated or Administrative Phase, and (3) the Integrative or Associative phase. There may be a fourth phase, which basically deals with how an organization comes to an end or transitions into a totally new initiative. I prefer to call each of these phases in the order by which they appear, rather than by specific labels. Labels like these have multiple connotations and may limit instead of enhance our understanding.

The Beginning

The very first phase of a growing organism is characterized by simplicity, single purpose, unity and a need to protect this vulnerable initiative from undue outside influences.

Differentiation

Each successive phase of development in biological and social systems becomes more complex and differentiated than the previous phase, and develops sub-systems within the whole.

Integration/Assimilation

Each successive phase of development assimilates and integrates the forms and functions of the previous phases and metamorphoses these into greater complexity and higher levels of sophistication.

Irreversibility

An organism or organization does not usually regress to previous phases. In the case of nature, reversion may take place as a result of catastrophic outside influences (For instance, forest fires may revert an entire region back from a mature forest to a meadow-like ecosystem.). In the life of the human soul, reversing back to earlier psychological stages turns into pathology.

Transitions

Any transition from one phase to the next is accompanied by tension or even chaos. There is a contraction after each phase before another expansion is possible. All living organisms alternate between expansion and contraction phases. It is not really possible for any transition to come in a seamless and gentle way. It always takes extra energy to break the inertia of what is already in place.

Recapitulation

Each successive "incarnation" of an organism briefly recapitulates the main thematic aspects of the previous phase. (The entire Waldorf curriculum is built on that principle. Each successive elementary grade touches upon cultural milestones of the past. Toward the end of their schooling, children should be ready to fully take their place in, and contribute to, the cultures of today. It is as if we have to pay tribute to the preceding cultures before we are in a position to enter new and unknown territory.)

Phases in Organizational Development

> Note: I think that governmental institutions, including military, and institutionalized religious movements appear to answer to the same developmental laws, as do business and social institutions, but manifested over much longer periods of time, possibly because these organizations and movements exist beyond the temporary control of an individual or group of individuals.

There is an interesting relationship between all these phases. Each phase has wonderful characteristics as well as a shadow or dark side. The shadows and lights are inextricably tied together; the one would cease to be if the other did not exist. Light could never be seen were it not for the dark against which it can contrast itself. This fact is a physical reality as well as a powerful metaphor for our human world and the organizations we create. It is the Yin Yang principle: at the tail end of each quality, its opposite asserts itself. And at the very center of each field its opposite quality resides.

The beginning and end of each phase is accompanied by uncertainty, crises and chaos. Margaret Wheatley (1992) points out,

> Dissipative structures demonstrate that disorder can be the source of order, and that growth is found in disequilibrium, not in balance.

But these moments also contain the greatest potential for new opportunity and creativity. More or less in the middle of each phase is the period of greatest stability and form. Institutions and organizations oscillate between either too little form (chaos) or too much form (bureaucracy). Ideology-based institutions tend to have less form, while larger businesses often operate under too much structure. But each of these extremes can also have elements of the other in it. For instance, I see in many non-profit organizations a very strong bias toward less structure (this allows for greater creativity), and yet they persist in following certain organizational concepts that haven't changed for generations.

The onset of the First Phase occurs as soon as an individual or small group decides to start an organization. This founding can be quite intentional or come as the natural outcome of people working together on a common cause. As soon as an organization is born, it adheres strictly to a whole set of characteristics. There rarely are exceptions. The length of this phase, as well as the other phases, can vary. The first period usually lasts from three to seven years.

First Phase

Opportunities:
There is a wonderful energy and enthusiasm and idealism connected with this phase. Innovation and novelty reign. It's like the birth of a child—innocence and joy. Joy in even the most challenging aspects of the work. Pain and tears—but it is good kind of pain, a pain that we want more of. Joyful sacrifice is the currency of the realm. Our needs to earn money or build a career or attend to family needs, etc., are subservient to survival of the organization. This usually means long hours of meeting until deep in the night and early morning study groups, because that is the only time available to all. *As with the parents of a young child, the founders or entrepreneurs hold a protective and sheltering gesture over their initiatives.* By the virtue of their strength and insight, the impossible becomes possible. We are intoxicated by the sheer euphoria of making a difference in the world.

The tasks, the vision and purpose are implicit and often embodied by the founders. There is a great flexibility to adapt to unforeseen circumstances and make do with the minimum of resources. The organizational structure is flat, meaning almost everyone interfaces with everyone else, and work is performed as the needs arise. We wear many hats all at once. Policies and procedures are hardly necessary because the tasks and responsibilities are straightforward, and if not, policies are invented on the spot and most likely forgotten afterwards. A genuine loyalty and gratitude toward the founders and their cause prevails, coupled with a dependence on their leadership. Any of the organizational characteristics in the First Phase are not only appropriate but also greatly needed to make the initiative stand on its own feet.

The purest form of the First Phase is manifested only in the first few years of an initiative. Soon after that, the demands of a growing organization increase in complexity.

On rare occasions, an overly conscientious person finds his way into a new initiative and, from the goodness of his heart, imagines every possible legal and financial liability the young organization might face in the near future. Subsequently, he writes up extensive policies to avoid these possible disasters all under the charge: Let's not re-invent the wheel.

But *in social and organizational life, for the most part wheels do indeed need to be re-invented.* Each phase of development needs to be experienced from the inside out. It would be silly to expect an infant, for instance, to forget about baby teeth but just go straight to the permanent set of teeth. Doing so would avoid a lot of grief and would be much more efficient. But life doesn't work that way. Somehow, for the sake of the ultimate development into a healthy human adult, children need to go through these stages. Woe is the day when some brilliant scientist figures out a chemical formula that would bypass the growing and shedding of baby teeth. At what terrible price would the child be spared the grief of teething?

Challenges:
Founders tend to have powerful personalities with strong ideas and ideals and are therefore less receptive to input, questioning, differing ideas, or collaboration from in or outside the organization. There are always exceptions, of course. On account of their creativity, they prefer to work with less structure (i.e. policies and procedures, clearly defined roles and responsibilities, committee structures, etc.), or work with structures that are amorphous, keeping the option to do whatever they see fit. This is not done out of malice but more from deeply held convictions of what is right and wrong for the organization. Even boards of these young initiatives are often handpicked friends and the founders. The former are more than happy to acquiesce to what has already been decided way before the meeting even takes place. There often is no true oversight or any meaningful dialogue among these governing bodies.

As we have seen in the collapse of the Enron Corporation, boards should play a vital role in being an internal monitoring agent, as well as being responsible for financial and legal matters. Instead we are finding out that most corporate boards are appointed and serve at the pleasure of the chief executives. Adding to this incestuous political conflict of interest is the fact that corporate board membership provides tremendous financial and prestige benefits to the appointee. These factors make it virtually impossible for a board to function as an independent voice, much to the detriment of the corporation and to all who depend on its success. Critique and oversight, so feared by most of us, would have saved this company from the collapse it suffered. Sadly, many corporate boards are nothing more than "good old boys" clubs.

Organizations, businesses and institutions take on the strengths and weaknesses of those who gave them birth. Their strengths shine most in the early years, while these same qualities often become hindrances in later years of the organization. It can even go deeper. Like sponges, organizations absorb the life themes and patterns of their founders in a profound way. It is as if their lives become externalized and projected on the screen of the organization. Personality traits that in larger work environments would get absorbed in the give-and-take among many coworkers and also by structural confines become amplified instead. The distinction blurs between personal issues of the founders and issues intrinsic to the organization. A crisis of identity ensues for both.

Transition to the Second Phase:
The average teenager can make little claim to a past record of achievement or of being reliable, but nevertheless steps forward and demands to be heard and seen. Likewise, the organization emancipates itself from those who brought it into existence. The success of the earlier phase guarantees the emergence of the Second Phase because of the increased complexity resulting from growth. It cannot be otherwise. Administrative functions and positions become more and more specialized and explicit. People with the necessary expertise in these fields are drawn to the organization. The same people seek greater stability and long-term viability for the organization as well as for themselves. No more sketching budgets on the back of an envelope. No more making decisions around the kitchen table. People require knowing how, when, and by whom decisions are made. Computer systems need to be networked. How about getting an answering machine? How about hiring a full-time secretary to meet people's inquiries—someone who can properly represent the organization to the outside world.

The organization begins to stand on its own somewhat awkward feet. The transition from the First Phase to the next can be traumatic. It is like a Greek tragedy. The audience and the players know the outcome but each step is nevertheless taken in the illusion that fate can be dodged. The Chorus echoes each tragic choice. Founders feel unappreciated, misinterpreted, and thrown by the wayside. I know of few exceptions to this scenario. Feelings get hurt. In most cases, the founders leave bewildered, hurt and resentful. Sometimes the wave of newcomers loses out in this classic power struggle. *Sometimes the founders can repulse the onslaught of new ideas and new people, like a body that rejects a transplanted organ.* Sometimes, the founders hold on for many additional years, but the spark is gone and the organization begins to grow stale.

Not that a new wave of people and ideas will necessarily guarantee a successful transition or a healthy growth into the next phase. But the alternative scenario of a graceful integration of the new with the old seems nearly impossible. It would require all parties to change their identity. And it is not just a question of individual people changing their relationship to the organizational transitions; these transitions take place with or without any one particular person.

Yet, there is a greater wisdom embedded in this tragic scenario. Often the old must fade away to make place for the new. Like booster rockets that power a space shuttle into orbit, only to be violently separated from their payload when no longer needed (tiny explosives are used to break the inertia between both bodies), so are the founders asked to basically sacrifice themselves twice: once in establishing the institution, and once in stepping back.

Often business entrepreneurs seem to have an innate knowledge of this principle, much more than those who work in the human service areas such as Waldorf schools. The former often specialize in starting businesses and leave the running of them up to others. They love being booster rockets and they will eagerly recycle themselves for the next exciting ride.

On the hopeful side, I have seen quite a number of situations in which the orbits of the founders and their erstwhile organizations eventually find equilibrium, but on a higher level. This reconciliation usually happens around significant milestones in the organization's biography. The circle of healing is then complete and people can get ready for the next challenge.

Second Phase

Opportunities:
The Second Phase is characterized by the diversification and specialization of functions and tasks, not to mention the mere increase in size of the organization. At last, the organization stands fully in the world. For those of us who had the privilege to assist at the birth of an initiative, there is no greater satisfaction than to see the organization come into its own. Roles and responsibilities are clear. People in the organization are fully accountable to each other and to the world around them. In the best sense of the word, professionalism is the norm in the organization. A much greater diversity of background and perspective is incorporated. Greater stability on all levels is obtained. Governing bodies stand in active dialogue with each other.

The organization is now fully visible to the outside world and recognized by it and interacting with it. Even when the institution is not quite at the level indicated above, all these elements are within its reach.

Challenges:
As a result of the increase in size (more people, more programs, more buildings, more paperwork, more regulations), it becomes much harder to maintain a sense of the totality and, more importantly, a sense of enthusiasm. Functional organs, like committees, form sub-committees. Administrative tasks can become so large and complex that additional staff is needed to meet the workload and answer the need for more expertise. Each department has its own organizational structure and staff, which in turn forms silos that are tall, narrow, and separated from the others. Communication and coordination among all the various working groups become increasingly difficult. It is easy for factions to arise. Turf battles ensue. Working groups feel isolated and separated from the rest. Judgments are made that

one particular contribution and function in the organization is more important than another (faculty versus staff, for instance, or part-time versus full-time employees). A hierarchy of perceived importance sets in. A bureaucracy develops for its own sake. What once was one whole now splinters into fragments.

In many business organizations, the downside of the Second Phase manifests itself in top-down decision-making processes within sharply defined and impersonal hierarchical structures. Somehow it is assumed that the rank and file will only perform their duties, or adhere to an ethical code, when closely controlled from the top. These power structures seem remnants of feudal times when human beings were less equipped to take personal responsibility for their actions. Leadership in this phase is more easily defined by position than inherent capacity to inspire.

For ideology-based organizations, the dragon shows itself most readily by tendencies opposite to the above: maintaining amorphous organizational structures, lack of defined decision-making processes, absence of leadership and transparent accountability.

An increase in available technologies (e-mail, faxes, instant messaging) does not necessarily remedy this splintering effect. Paradoxically, communication can exacerbate the sense of isolation. The nature of the communication can be impersonal, or reach such volume as to overwhelm. Members of some large corporations now receive hundreds of e-mails per day. How is one to mentally scan, prioritize, and maintain a sense of purpose in this maze of information? I cannot imagine. So often when people tell me there is a lack of communication, I find there is too much instead. Too much background noise, as when you are forced to sleep in a cheap motel situated next to a truck stop. This excess noise is true for larger as well as smaller organizations.

The greatest danger, besides the impersonal and fractured nature of the Second Phase, can be a clouding of the original meaning and purpose of the initiative. Who knows what is going on? What do all these forms have to do with our profession anyway? Will we ever move beyond the unhelpful patterns and themes that we have seen come and go for years? Many companies and schools may spend millions on developing long-term plans and mission statements to infuse the organization with new life. In most cases these plans either end up in a file cabinet or, even when they are published, have little effect. Spending most of its resources on itself, the organization focuses on itself. This phase is similar to the phases of early and middle adulthood where the need to support, promote and strengthen self, family and career is paramount. The vast majority of all businesses and institutions hover somewhere in the middle of the Second Phase.

Transition from Second Phase to Third Phase:
It is small wonder that many people would prefer staying fixed in a pseudo-First Phase rather than face the shadows of the Second Phase. The Second Phase, however, is not only unavoidable; its gifts are absolutely key to the ultimate success and therefore survival of the organization—no matter its present size, mission, profitability or level of idealism. The challenge of the Second Phase is to renew itself from within. This can only be done if its people are willing to step beyond what is comfortable and familiar. Unlike the inevitable change from the First to the Second Phase, a transition to the Third Phase is never automatic! *In many ways the exciting as well as the daunting challenge of the Third Phase is that it is ever to be created anew.* Glimpses and elements can be present in the Second Phase—and for that matter also the First Phase—from which we get an idea of what lies ahead, and from which we can gain inspiration.

Third Phase

This phase is difficult to describe because organizations move in and out of this phase, or they only exhibit aspects at a time. The Third Phase can be characterized as more a process of working rather than a state of being. A mature organization is an organization in which there is a culture of continuous learning and a commitment to apply what is learned (Senge 1990). It does not matter whether people make mistakes or whether events come to pass that negatively impact the organization. In fact, mistakes and difficulties provide much greater opportunities for growth than what happens when everything is perfect. How many institutions do you know in which this culture of continuous learning is alive?

The Third Phase is basically analogous to that of mature self-aware human beings. These people are integrated into the world, aware of their strengths and limitations, confident, focused, and clear of their wants in relation to obligations and dreams.

Everything we have come to know and respect in the areas of leadership, organizational structures, vision, effective ways of working, requires a fundamental paradigm shift in order to enter this later phase. Nothing is given except certain principles of operation rather than pre-conceived ideas of how something "ought to be." The paradigm shift that is taking place in the physical and theoretical sciences must penetrate not only how we think about our organizations and social life, but also how we act in them. We have now come to a point where, in order to describe this Third Phase, a much deeper exploration of social and organizational life becomes necessary.

Let's start with one of the shadows of the Second Phase: the loss of organizational cohesiveness among all members of the organization. Mature working communities develop clarity of vision and unity of action—in the midst of highly complex and diversified functions—by a continuous process of feedback and participation of *all* its constituents. *No matter how well-intentioned and experienced a leader or leadership group may be, vision and mission can no longer be meaningful if they are formulated and promoted by the few.* Paradoxically, unity of vision and action can only be derived when the most diverse stakeholders of the organization are involved. All who have a stake in the well-being of the organization must develop vision, mission and be involved in long-term planning for the organization. To quote Margaret Wheatley:

> We know that the best way to build ownership is to give over the creation process to those who will be charged with its implementation. It doesn't work to just ask people to sign on when they haven't been involved in the design process, when they haven't experienced the plan as a living, breathing thing. As we know from quantum logic, it is impossible to expect any plan or idea to be real to employees, if they do not have the opportunity to personally interact with it.

And Jeffrey McCollum (Star Throwers Associates and The Robert K. Greenleaf Center):

> We live in a most interesting world. We are working in a time when concepts of organization and leadership are in full ferment: the assumption and practices that led to the success of the bureaucratic model (Second Phase) are disintegrating. A collective effort is on the way to redefine how work is done and how organizations are led. Organization design seems to come from the outside in rather than from the top down. This requires the full participation—physically, emotionally and intellectually—of all people in our organizations.

At the beginning of the organization it was one person or a very small group that conceived and brought the initiative to birth. But in this later phase of development, the continuous renewal and direction of the initiative now comes from all corners and levels of the organization. In other words, gestation and early life of the organization came from the center, while further development comes from the periphery.

When an object is thrown into a pond, the concentric circles ripple out to the periphery, and once these circles reach the periphery, they revert back toward the center but in richer and more intricate patterns. So too, the Third Phase is characterized by the most intricate and beautiful and ever-changing organizational forms. These organizational forms and structures alter according to the specific needs of the moment.

This principle of reaching out to the farthest corners of the institution by involving all of its constituents can be counter-intuitive to many in human service organizations and in the corporate world. So often I hear people maintain that only a core group that has made a long-term commitment to the institution can speak for its future direction and identity. This may have been the case some generations ago and in a different cultural context. But not so in the Third Phase, nor in the realities of present-day Western culture. The true essence or Being of an organization can only come to expression by way of the human encounter and continuous dialogue among all members and interested parties.

There are proven methodologies that can ensure productive cycles of feedback and full participation of all constituents. I will describe these methodologies later.

Once an organization reaches this level of sophistication by providing full disclosure of its inner workings and opportunities for informed participation by all its stakeholders, each member of that community assumes an important obligation. *A conscious relationship between the community and the individual requires a reciprocal commitment. Now members can no longer sit back and criticize the organization without acknowledging they are co-creators of reality.* The "them" dissolves into the "us." Dictated by outer and inner circumstances, each one of us can only contribute according to ability and availability.

Some of us might be attending two or three meetings per year, while others are in a position to contribute significant volunteer time and expertise, while still others are employed by the organization. All these different levels of involvement do not change our status as co-creators of our institutions.

The Third Phase has a lot to do with recognizing and embracing paradox. Life has many paradoxes. Paradox exists in the earlier phases also, but its existence can be drowned out in the flood of needs to survive and grow. In "In Praise of Paradox" Julian Rappaport (1981) wrote,

> We stand in a turmoil of contradictions without having the faintest idea how to handle them—law/freedom, rich/poor, right/left, love/hate—the list seems endless. Paradox lives and moves in this realm; it is the art of balancing opposites in such a way that they do not cancel each other but shoot sparks of light across their points of polarity. It looks at our desperate either/ors and tells us they are really both/ands—that life is larger than any of our concepts and can, if we let it, embrace our contradictions.

Each biological and social organism has an identity that distinguishes it from the rest of the world. An identity or Being can only survive if it has a boundary (skin) that functions as a gatekeeper between what is inside and what is outside. In the earlier phases of development it is important to protect the organism from the outside (even though the organism draws sustenance from the outside onto itself), so that it has time to strengthen itself and then take its place among all other entities. But in the Third Phase these boundaries become more and more permeable. By actively interfacing with its surroundings, an identity actually strengthens itself instead of being dissolved into something other than itself. A paradox.

Now the organization can and must *associate* with other organizations by entering into time and task-limited agreements. In the business world, the practice of outsourcing is an example of entering into association with other businesses. There are many examples in the human service and public sectors: land trusts and consumer/distributor/producer associations. There are associations of environmental groups, ethnic groups, developers, landowners, and local industries. Private and public schools associate with home-schooling groups. The list goes on and on.

Prior to their associative work, each of these groups had diverse and often conflicting agendas. But in each of these examples, the individual identities and missions of these institutions and groups are actually expanded and deepened by their association with others.

Fourth Phase

I think there is a Fourth Phase at work. This phase has to do with completion and ending. Seldom do people in charge of an organization recognize the signs that its products or services have become obsolete until it is too late. But far-sighted members of organizations should in some way anticipate or at least accept the possibility for a proper transition for ending or re-inventing the mission. This takes vision and courage.

The associative nature of the third level organization, as it turns toward its relationship with the outside world, also pertains to its internal workings. Smaller mandated groups will easily form and dissolve according to need. These groups or individuals have time-limited tasks with very specific desired outcomes. There always is a great tendency to hold on to ideas of how an organization should look from a structural point of view. These structures, while appropriate at one time, can be a hindrance at other times. The only structure in a non-profit, tax-exempt institution that is required by law is a Board. All other governing bodies are discretionary and can be arranged according to need.

I do not imply that structures (governing bodies, standing committees, reporting responsibilities, leadership groups, etc.) can come and go at will. The mature organization has certain principles that give these structures permanency. Permanency is of course necessary. But I find that strongly held, preconceived ideas of what ought to be, even before an institution is founded, can be a greater danger. These preconceived ideas are abstract ideas that may have little to do with the particular mission, or geographic, demographic, and historical conditions in which the organization is placed.

Instead, the people in a Third Phase organization can look at roles and functions that need to be in place for a well-run operation, and design structures around these needs. For instance, if a certain group has an oversight function to see to the flow of information, this group need not also be in charge of making key decisions. These two functions would be separated out if that were deemed necessary. We make many assumptions based on autocratic and hierarchical models.

4

Leadership in the Third Phase

Leadership styles change fundamentally in this phase. While in the earlier phases leadership was still vested in a few individuals, now many carry this function. There is an equation at work here:

> To the extent that more and more members in the work-community take full responsibility for the life of the organization, to that extent traditional forms of leadership become irrelevant.

Peter Block (*The End of Leadership* 1994, 1997) has an interesting take on the relationship between leaders and citizens (i.e. members of a community):

> The paradox is that we have created a world so dependent on the centrality of leadership that citizens and employees have developed a learned *dependency*. If you ask citizens and employees what they want, they most often affirm the need for a kinder monarch. People seek the safety and comfort of someone at the top keeping the vision alive, promising a safe and prosperous tomorrow.

and,

> Without getting lost in definition, citizenship is our agreement to receive rights and privileges from the community and, in so doing, to pay for them through our willingness to live within certain boundaries and act in the interest of the whole. At

> the core of citizenship is the desire to care for the well-being of the larger institution, be it an organization, a neighborhood, or a country. This requires accountability. This is the purchase price of our freedom.

and,

> The trap we fall into in the face of passivity is to believe the solution is better leadership. Avoiding responsibility, compliance, and caution on the part of employees and citizens is a bigger problem than control and self-centeredness on the part of "leaders." The solution is not to keep trying to create better leaders, it is to explore how to become accountable citizens.

and,

> The focus on the leader is a collective escape from taking responsibility. A culture of accountability will come from turning our attention away from leaders and committing ourselves to creating a deeper sense of community and citizenship.

Laurens van der Post agrees, "the way we glamorize leaders is a way of escaping from owning our responsibility for the world we have created."

In the Third Phase, the concept and practice of leadership radically changes from dependency to co-responsibility. There are of course always conditions under which control and command leadership is still essential. After all, when firefighters are in the process of performing lifesaving rescue missions, a clear chain of command with strict orders are a must. There are many other examples, mostly to do with first-order safety issues, where precise leadership is required. But even in these conditions, frontline people are often faced with realities not accessible to those that lead from a distance.

> A mature organization has evolved to a point where it has successfully transitioned from top-down leadership to clearly mandated groups and individuals.

The concept and the need for leadership is changing. Usually, leadership is seen as telling other people what to do—through charisma or power—or pointing the directions others or the organization should go. These are valid attributes of leadership. But today leadership means so much more. Leadership can come from any one person who is in any number of roles. Situational leadership comes about when the need of a particular moment is met by a person with initiative. This can be in small matters, as in helping to paraphrase a point made by another person in a conversation, or as big as in helping to articulate a clearer vision for the organization. It can be in providing direction, helping to solve problems, supporting others in their work or in mentoring, and so forth.

Ethical leaders lead from behind the scenes, or from the bottom up; they often are invisible. When we speak of informal leadership, we describe a similar experience—the capacity of the organization to create the leadership that best suits its needs at the time. We may fail to honor (or recognize) these leaders more formally, trapped as we are in a hierarchical structure that is non-adaptive, but in the Third Phase of a well-functioning organization, we know who the leader is and why he or she needs to be there. Max De Pree calls this "roving leadership, the indispensable people in our lives who are there when we need them."

In American culture, and most other cultures, we have a love/hate relationship to leaders. We yearn for them and as soon as they are firmly in place, we seek to undermine them. This reality alone should give us a hint that the traditional role of the leader no longer applies to modern humanity. Yet, we are so entrenched in our traditional organization structures, that this collective oppositional/compliant behavior on our part escapes our notice.

Leaders who are placed in institutional defined leadership roles would be wise to avoid this trap and dedicate their efforts to placing greater and greater responsibility on the rest of the community. That's true servant leadership. Followers turn into leaders when they take responsibility for the health and welfare of the entire organization and community, instead of placing themselves in the victim role by blaming those who appear to have power over them.

5

Living and Working in the Third Phase

The future of the Waldorf movement—any movement for that matter—will entirely depend on our ability to collaborate and form associations with organizations and individuals who share aspects of our mission. No longer can we survive with an attitude of emphasizing our differences from the rest of the world. Our central task will be to seek what we share in common with countless other organizations and individuals.

This shift in attitude could be quite difficult for many in an organization. Many spiritually- and ideologically-based movements are embedded in a culture of "for members only." Most spiritual movements are that way. They are exclusive rather than inclusive in nature. Traditionally, the path to enlightenment was an individual quest. Specific spiritual practices were entirely geared to individual developmental needs. A student had to meet strict conditions of soul and character before the student was deemed ready. All these requirements were in place because they answered to the realities of the times. But Rudolf Steiner (1993) made it clear that the path of modern enlightenment and initiation should no longer be hidden from public life. Indeed, the path of modern enlightenment is primarily through the interaction and relationship with others in social and professional life.

All too often I hear the phrase and encounter the attitude: We are different. If we believe our background and mission to be different—and therefore not easily understood by others—we are likely to set up organizational structures designed to protect that uniqueness. A greater and greater separation between "us" and "them" ensues. We have a tendency to want to create "islands of culture" in a sea of materialism and other opposing forces. But islands do not survive in social life. Even if we wanted to, it is an illusion to think that we can place ourselves apart from the rest of humanity. On every level of material, social and spiritual life, our spiritual development is dependent on the well-being of every other person on earth.

The core of Manichean teachings (Lievegoed 1992) emphasizes this principle of our interdependence on each other for our development, and therefore is most applicable to the Third Phase in organizational life and indeed modern-day consciousness. According to Professor Lievegoed's interpretation, there are at least three major Manichean principles:

First, *each light casts a shadow*. If you do the good, you will inevitably create its shadow. A candle lit in a dark room will cast shadows that were not seen before. It is as if the light pushes away the darkness, which then makes the surroundings even darker. After all, darkness has to go somewhere; it doesn't just disappear into nothingness. If, for instance, you worked well with others on a task, the group will be faced with greater and greater tasks as time passes. As a group member, I have experienced that dynamic a number of times. This may be the reason why so many of us have, on a subconscious level, resistance to change. We would rather maintain the status quo because we feel that more difficult work is waiting around the corner.

Related to the first principle is the second that states, *our shadows—and evil in general—must be met with gentleness*. So much of what we hear over the airwaves from officials in governmental and religious institutions is that evil must be fought at all costs and that evil is "out there" and has little to do with us. Evil is externalized and placed on the shoulders of others. How convenient! Of course, in the extreme some people may well deserve the label of evil. But Manichean thought attempts to take ownership of the vexing question of evil, in the recognition that criminal tendencies lurk in my soul and the souls of each of us. Evil is not to be defeated, because it cannot be defeated by us humans. In fact, as is the case with shadows, we make evil stronger by fighting it. All we human beings can do is to take situations that are evil and work with them in such a way that good may come out of it. It is with a certain amount of humility and with inner strength that we must face what is most frightening in our institutions and ourselves. By naming what scares us most, we weaken its power over us.

Thirdly, *each step in our own inner development will mean that others will be left behind and somehow pay a price for it.* This principle may be harder to accept as true. But it rings true to me especially if I consider the question in reverse. Can anyone advance without standing on the shoulders of others? Or, what have others sacrificed—and will have to sacrifice—for me so that I can advance? What services and gifts and material resources have come my way so that I can take a step in my development? I therefore assume an obligation toward the world, which is to turn around and place what I have gained back in service to others.

The Manichean principles are truly social principles. And social life pertains to organizational life. And organizational life is subject to the same developmental laws as human beings are. The Third Phase in organizational development represents assuming an expanded mission by forming associations with other organizations in service to the greater good.

Transparency and Accountability

A sister quality of association is the quality of transparency. The one cannot exist without the other. The need for transparency cannot be overemphasized. A mature and fully established organization is transparent in all respects.

Nothing is hidden from anyone. Transparency is the base criterion for all decision making. People will know by whom and why decisions are made. Each decision and arrangement will stand the rigors of scrutiny by internal as well as external governing bodies, agencies and individuals. Are our practices consistent with the highest professional standards? For that matter, are we transparent to ourselves as members of an organization?

Keep in mind we are now in the Third Phase of development in which all stakeholders (meaning, every person who has a relationship to the organization) can experience the organization as transparent and have had the opportunity to interface with it. Therefore the organization can truly act on behalf of each community member.

It goes without saying that financial transactions and bookkeeping should be consistent with official accounting practices for transparency's sake. In terms of gifting, I run into quite a few cases where donors choose to remain anonymous. There are multiple and very legitimate reasons for a donor's request to remain anonymous. This is a time-honored tradition. But in the long run these arrangements obscure the nature of relationships. The lack of transparency easily sets barriers between people. Some people know, others do not know. It is no better when financial or legal institutions act as intermediary; in fact, that can make matters worse because of the extra layers of relationships added. In either case, the situation limits unfiltered information exchange, hence freedom of informed choice and the ability for all parties to take full responsibility for their actions.

I know that many of you reading this may strenuously disagree with my views on this matter. We should be pragmatic enough to make the necessary compromises if it absolutely has to be. That's life. But there is a principle at stake here. And the principle is that we live in an age where nothing must be hidden from view. That holds in spiritual matters as well as material matters. In the worst instances, anything that is hidden lends itself to confusion and manipulation. For both donor and recipient it is a question of learning to gradually bring their relationship to light.

When a donor decides to remain anonymous while also placing restrictive conditions on a gift, we have entered an untenable situation from any perspective (conditions for matching funds requirements excluded). Now the will of the donor reaches way into the decision-making process with additional layers obscuring the underlying reality. For one, it places on those who are in the know the obligation to act on behalf of an unknown entity without the ability to disclose assumptions, motivations or rationale. In cases of anonymity, a gift with strings attached is not a gift, it is an acquisition. The donor buys influence.

The most difficult of all scenarios is when donors demand anonymity and are also members of the recipient community, especially if the donor is a staff, faculty or board member. In the beginning years of an institution this happens quite a lot. Maybe in the first year or two of the organization such circumstances cannot always be avoided. I have known about situations where the person is the donor at one moment and in the next is part of a group making decisions about how to appropriate the money, while other members are unaware of the dual relationship. Even when assuming the best of motivations and intentions to help the organization, such arrangements lead to an unavoidable conflict of interest.

By far the best is when donors can disclose their identity and their motivations for the gift. Then the recipient organization, on behalf of all its members, can in freedom accept the terms, re-negotiate, or decline the offer. The donor is an equal stakeholder among equal stakeholders. Everyone is left in freedom to act while honoring our mutual commitments.

Part Two

Tools for Organizational Change

6

The Mandate System in Concept and Practice

The Oxford American Dictionary defines mandate as "an official order or commission to do something," or (law) "a commission by which a party is entrusted to perform a service," or "the authority to carry out a policy or course of action." According to the dictionary, the origin of the word mandate dates back to the 16th century, from the Latin *mandatum*, 'something commanded,' neuter past particle of *mandare*, from *manus* 'hand' + *dare* 'give.'

The concept of a mandate is usually found within a political context, as in an electoral mandate. If we stay strictly with the definitions from the dictionary, these are an apt description of the use and purpose of mandates in an organization. In addition to that, the mandate system as described below is primarily a decentralized management tool that allows larger and more complex organizations in the Third Phase to effectively carry out their mission with full accountability. As such, this methodology represents a departure from the usual top-down management practices that one finds in nearly every business and altruistically based institution.

Why should we work with a decentralized management system rather than with a clear chain of command driven from the top down? Certainly, the latter approach, when working at its best, has clear advantages:

a. Usually, leaders hold a clearer vision for the future direction and mission of the organization.

b. With the more traditional leadership model (usually vested in one person), decisions can be made efficiently and expediently.
c. Leaders can more easily be held accountable.
d. There is no confusion on who speaks for the organization.
e. There can be little question on who provides guidance and instruction in all aspects of daily management and long-term planning.
f. There can be little confusion on the organizational structure and decision-making authorities.

The mandate system as it is currently understood and practiced does ensure a greater level of participation, and therefore ownership in the welfare of the institution. It can lack, however, some of the above-mentioned benefits, which can leave people frustrated but still intrigued with the promise of new ways of working. Many Waldorf-related institutions somehow oscillate back and forth between these two models and therefore cannot reap the benefits of either one.

The Case for a Properly Implemented Mandate System

As a prerequisite, organizations must have entered, or be near the Third Phase of development as described in the earlier chapters.

1. The most capable and benevolent of leaders, or even a leadership group, can no longer embody the wisdom or managerial and technical skills to lead a complex organization into the future by themselves. Individual leadership shortcomings inevitably become the shortcomings of the entire organization unless we access the collective resources of all its members.

2. Generally, consensus incorporates the best thinking of everyone.

3. Consensus helps people to stay away from adversarial attitudes.

4. The health and continued success of an organization is the business of all its members and constituents. Even the spiritual life in an institution is the business of all—novice or not—who voluntarily seek to contribute and take responsibility.

5. No vision, mission or long-term plan can ever be successfully implemented without the participation and commitment of those who are affected by it. The reader must know plenty of examples where organizations spent copious amounts of money and human resources on developing mission statements and master plans, only to have these plans end up ignored and filed away.

6. People are seeking participation, ownership and community, whatever their individual circumstances and skills. For some that may mean minimal involvement, while for others it may represent a full-time occupation. Whatever the level of involvement, all members of the community deserve to have their voices heard and have an important part to contribute.

Board governance

In this new mandate system, board governance retains its traditional role with the only caveat that all decisions are the result of continuous dialogue with their constituents. The board does not get involved in the daily management of the institution.

- Their efforts are concentrated on seeing the big picture.
- They are the guardians of the *vision and mission* of the organization.

- With *full* and continuous participation of the entire community, they develop the *policies and procedures* that provide the parameters within which the mandate groups operate.
- With *full* and continuous participation of the entire community, they develop long-term plans and goals.
- They have particular responsibility for the financial health of the organization. That includes fundraising.
- They have particular responsibility for the legal aspects of running an organization, *and* the board ensures that ethical standards and practices on all levels are observed and enforced.
- The board helps parcel out the *implementation* of its policies to mandate groups and individuals.
- Finally, they help foster the spiritual life in the organization by way of example through study and continuous self-improvement practices.

Never should any group set itself above the rest of the organization by asserting that they have moral authority over others because they are united behind a particular worldview or spiritual practice.

Leadership functions within an organization

Instead of the traditional role of the director or some executive council making the key decisions in all departments of the organization, in this mandate system leaders assume a coordinating and facilitating role.

- Their efforts are, like that of the board, concentrated on seeing the big picture. By taking the larger view, they can more easily identify gaps or bottlenecks in the information flow and task distribution.

- They help facilitate processes and arbitrate differences among people and policy inconsistencies.
- Together with the board, they are responsible for the implementation of the vision and mission by assigning tasks to mandate groups and individuals.
- They help develop the policies and procedures that guide every action and decision made in the mandate groups—policies and procedures on hiring and firing, evaluation, personnel, programs and curriculum, facility maintenance and new construction, finance, administration, etc.
- They may mandate a contact person to interface with constituents and field official inquiries.
- They help foster the spiritual life in the organization by way of example.

The mandate and mandate groups

In short, the mandate groups act on behalf of the leadership groups. Included in the mandate are very strict guidelines on timely research, proposals, decision making, reporting and accountability (see below).

Outwardly, the array of mandate groups is similar to the committee structures one finds in non-profit organizations. But now these groups each hold an essential piece of governing responsibility usually concentrated in the hands of the few. Besides their eminently practical use, I think mandates have a deeply spiritual element in them:

> The archetypal gesture of the mandate is that a governing group or individual *empowers* and *entrusts* another group or individual to act on their behalf.

In other words, a group bestows part of its power on another group. This free deed of trust and empowerment has the effect of making the recipients be more than what they would have been otherwise; which in turn greatly enriches the entire organization including the governing group. By giving power away, power multiplies in a healthy way and throughout the organization. One could say:

> The rightful exercise of power is to prepare others to assume it on your behalf.

Rudolf Steiner gives this wonderful and inspiring invocation (German original published in *Wahrspruchworte,* GA 40, p. 136):

> Seek the real practical life, but seek it in a way that it does not blind you for the Spirit working in it.
>
> Seek the Spirit, but do not seek it in spiritual greed, from spiritual egotism,
>
> But look for it because you want to apply it unselfishly in practical life, in the material world.
>
> Make use of the ancient principle: Spirit is never without matter, matter never without Spirit.

Whenever mandates are created, governing groups may do well to remind themselves of the lofty purpose of this task. In fact, the enthusiasm and energy so characteristic of the early phases of an initiative can now be consciously infused in the Third Phase, when running an organization can appear so arduous. The underlying principle at work is:

> In the Third Phase, the underlying principle at work is that governing bodies assert less and less direct control over the daily administrative management of the organization; instead they concentrate their efforts on the long-term mission, identity and health of the organization.

The process of creating a mandate is straightforward and rational enough. However, in spite of the beauty of this system, you may find it difficult to institutionalize it in your organization. There always are entrenched conditions in any organization that work against necessary changes. This is just a fact of life to which all of us contribute. Nevertheless, if the following concepts and procedures are meticulously performed the chances for success are great.

While the governing groups—Boards and/or Executive Councils—are charged with creating and staffing mandated groups, it can be very helpful for the membership to be chosen in full community meetings at a time when the committee structures are set for the year. This gives an opportunity for all who have an active role in the organization to provide constructive input and involvement and assume, thereby, greater responsibility for the totality. When we speak of an institutional vision and long-term planning in a well-established organization (Third Phase), this should never be the exclusive province of the governing bodies.

At the outset, a distinction must be made between *constitutional mandates* and *operational mandates*.

A constitutional mandate is one derived from the Articles of Incorporation and Bylaws of the institution. These mandates pertain to the governing bodies and core standing committees of the organization. Their mandates are *permanent* and *multifaceted* in nature. (Besides the Board and some type of

Executive Council or President, many Bylaws also designate a Finance Committee as a standing committee.)

When there is a question about the constitutional mandates of these standing governing bodies, the Articles and Bylaws should provide the answer. If there is no clear description of these mandates, or if there are conflicting descriptions, the Bylaws will have to be amended according to prescribed procedures to address the inconsistencies.

Do not bypass this important condition—namely, absolute clarity and consistency in the roles and responsibilities of the governing bodies as articulated in the Articles of Incorporation and its Bylaws. The Articles and Bylaws are the bedrock of the organization. Any inconsistency will result in endless confusion and a faulty mandate system.

An operational mandate is mostly singular in task and limited in duration. This type of mandate is primarily used for groups and individuals that have specific tasks to perform and/or decisions to make on behalf of a governing body or bodies.

> Note: It is not easy for most of us today to truly empower other people to exercise power and responsibility on our behalf. Somehow we feel that if proposals and decisions are not identical to what we would have done, the institution will suffer irreparable harm and never survive the mistakes. Such is the illusion under which most of us labor. To gradually wean us from this illusion, schools and other institutions would do well to set smaller mandates and to practice this process over and over again until the benefits to the organization and to ourselves become evident and self re-enforcing. We should learn to consciously and freely delegate responsibility to others without taking it back later on when it doesn't suit our purposes.

General Guidelines and Principles

As stated above, a mandate is a grant of authority by the governing bodies empowering a group or individual to act, research, or make proposals. There is, therefore, always a reporting responsibility from the mandated group or individual to the authorizing body.

• *In all that you do, publicize in advance a clear description of the mandate, the selection process, membership criteria and number of members.* When governing bodies are about to implement the creation of mandates, they should always publish their intent to the wider community. It is important that the community is kept informed on all organizational arrangements, even if only a few are directly impacted by the arrangement. In a Third Phase institution, full disclosure is the guiding norm.

• *Make sure that people know when and with whom a final decision is made.* In community meetings, the ideal approach is to make the final decision on membership selection right there and then so that the community can affirm the decision. Once a mandate group is operational, decisions might not only come toward the end of its mandate, but interim decisions might be required to complete the mandate. In many cases, governing bodies seek research and recommendations from mandated groups rather than decision making. However, as stated above, governing groups should concentrate their efforts on long-term goals and policies, not day-to-day management. Therefore, governing groups would be wise to delegate greater responsibility for decision making to mandate groups.

• *To obtain a balance of capacities in a mandate group, it is of much greater importance that individual members have the required skills rather than that they belong to a certain constituency of the organization*. Too often I find a tendency to seek representational membership at the expense of capacity and availability. If it is important that governing bodies be closely informed of developments in the proceedings of the mandate group, clarify that in the reporting responsibility. The greater danger is that governing groups seek to keep too close tabs on the proceedings instead of giving too free rein.

• *People cannot nominate themselves*. Whether in community meetings or governing group meetings, people should not volunteer to assume membership on committees. To be asked to serve is so much more empowering and affirming than volunteering. In the latter case, you are never fully sure that you have the support of others.

• *Each participant can only nominate one person to the position*. (This is done so that an open and full participation by all can be achieved.) This guideline pertains to community meetings, not necessarily to governing groups, although the latter may want to keep as close to this principle as possible.

• *Never allow absentee voting or secret balloting*. This greatly undermines the integrity of the group process and the trust that we have to cultivate among ourselves.

• *It is very helpful for the nominating person to give at least two reasons for the nomination.*

• *After all nominees are nominated, each nominee indicates his/her willingness to serve or not, and one or two reasons for acceptance or withdrawal.*

• *A mandate group needs to include only those who have jurisdiction over the task at hand. If a group has a member who is peripheral to the task or, worse, refers to the authority (insight/participation) of non-members in executing the mandate, the group loses its ability to fulfill its mandate*. In such a case, the group should be dismantled and reconstituted to include only those who ought to be there. (The reader should pay special attention to this principle because it is all too often violated in the course of daily work.)

Basic Components of a Mandate

1. Succinct description of the task

I cannot overemphasize the need for a very succinct and well-documented description of the task. The delegating body would do well to use all the time necessary to formulate and agree on the task. Any short-circuited process or open-ended description will inevitably result in spending much more energy and much more time afterwards. Write the task down (a paragraph or two should suffice), read it and re-read it until it is crystal clear and everybody is in full agreement. The task usually consists of fact-finding and/or making proposals and/or making decisions. A mandate could also be centered on a function, for instance, mediating a conflict.

2. Reporting responsibility

Make clear and document to whom and when and how (orally or in writing) the mandate group reports.

3. Decision-making authority and proposal making

If the mandate includes decision-making authority, we should be extremely clear and have it documented when and how decisions can be made. If this clarity exists prior to granting the mandate, then no one should second-guess or question the decision and the outcome. There is nothing more demoralizing and destructive to the people and health of the organization than to undo, second-guess, or plainly undermine decisions that were made under previously agreed processes and criteria. I truly believe that the health and success of an organization depends on how well decisions are adhered to and implemented. Any decision that is later contradicted weakens the life of the organization, and everyone in it, to the point of paralysis.

In addition, even if a mandate group was only asked to make recommendations, these recommendations should weigh *much* heavier in the debate than ones that come from those who were not part of the mandate group. When in doubt, or when no clear consensus can be reached, always give much greater deference to those who did the research and legwork on the issue.

4. Time line of when the task and the interim steps are to be completed

A proper mandate has a very specific time line for completion. If the completion date is exceeded, then the authorizing body must consent to another targeted completion date. A mandate must always be time-limited, usually no longer than a year in duration. A limited time frame and limited scope of the task helps in finding qualified individuals to serve with energy and commitment. After the task has been completed, the mandate can always be renewed if necessary, instead of making renewal automatic.

5. Criteria for membership and terms of service

It is essential to clarify and document who are eligible to serve, how many members are needed, and the length of time of service. Volunteering for key positions is usually not helpful. The governing group that decides on the mandate should be clear on the general criteria and identify specific people who may qualify. Make this as open a process as possible. Let the light of day shine on this process. When nominating a member, specify the reasons why he or she is a good candidate. The candidate has the freedom, of course, to decline. In either case, the nominee should be specific as to why he or she wants to accept the nomination, and also specify the strengths and weaknesses that he or she may bring to the task. All expectations and reservations should be clearly expressed by all sides and, when needed, addressed.

The reason for being so explicit and detailed in why a certain member is deemed qualified to serve, and why this member has chosen to accept or reject the position is, that it brings full consciousness into the act. It is as if the organization cultivates its "ego power" (in anthroposophical parlance). Being this explicit and detailed in nominating a candidate and in accepting the position also helps to further clarify the mandate.

Once the group has been selected and convened, it should have a frank discussion and decide if additional input or clarification is needed. The chair may either be chosen by the mandated group or by the delegating body. How the chair is chosen should be clarified as the mandate is formulated. I recommend the mandated group choose its own chair.

6. Selection Process

There are three possible scenarios for selection and approval:

a. Nomination and selection take place within a community meeting of all who have an active role in the organization.

b. A nominating committee is established and selects a slate that then is approved in the community meeting or by the governing body.

c. Nominations in writing are solicited for subsequent approval by the governing group.

One or more of the governing bodies should set the mandate and determine criteria for membership and do the candidate selection. However, I find it far more effective to select membership for these mandates in open community meetings comprised of capable and willing volunteers and staff members. These meetings are preferably held at the start or end of a calendar or work year. This has a fourfold benefit:

- The entire work community has in front of it the full scope of tasks to be performed for the next 12 months.
- Candidates can assess and prioritize where their energies, capacities and experience might be of greatest use.
- Selection can be done with the full spectrum of qualified candidates available.
- The final results can be affirmed and endorsed by everyone present.

Just think of the power and energy that will be generated by this method! Certainly, in the course of a year, new mandates might come about or old ones might need to be amended. This would not necessarily require a full community meeting.

If you want to select membership for more than one committee at a time, read all mandates and membership criteria at the beginning of the selection process. This enables people to take the totality into account once the nominating process starts. You may even choose the membership of more than one committee simultaneously, so that people have to prioritize their thinking.

I have chosen a *voting* procedure rather than working by *consensus*. I do not think that seeking consensus in a large group for this task is necessary. At the end of this process, each and every participant is asked to give his or her approval of the final outcome (slate). Since the process was transparent, fair and involved full participation, you will most often discover that unanimous consent is obtained—consensus.

If qualified members cannot be found, or the same people find themselves serving on many committees at the same time, it may be that the organization is overextending itself with too many committees. This usually happens when:

- from prior experiences groups and individuals are not really empowered and entrusted to do work on behalf of the rest, and/or
- leadership group(s) are confused about their role or lack a common vision. As mentioned above, in this case it is best to start with smaller pilot projects so that the organization can practice and gain confidence in the process.

If there are more committees than members to serve, combine certain committee functions.

7. Fine-tuning

Once the membership and the task have been agreed upon, the operational group or individual should work with the mandate in the best way they can and be given a chance early on in the process to suggest minor changes, if needed. This is done because there is no substitute for experience gained "in the field." The people closest to the action often gain insights and can make suggestions that may have been overlooked in the original design of the mandate.

> Walk a fine line between too much rigidity and too much flexibility in amending the mandate once it is set.

8. Process for soliciting input from constituents during the term of the mandate

It is very important to realize that part of the mandate includes how, and how often, the group should seek input and information from individuals and groups in the organization. I call these "input loops." This is a key element in the process. I would suggest that in most cases the group should be expected to seek input once or twice during the term of their mandate (depending on the complexity of the task), and to submit preliminary proposals for feedback and further input. When input is requested, give it freely without undue expectation that your comments and ideas will be reflected in the final results of the mandated group. Once again a very delicate balance must be reached between turning too often to the wider community or governing group, or not enough, so that the committee and its work become invisible to the rest in the organization.

It can easily happen that a committee gets stuck in its deliberations or is unable to make a final determination, or realizes that the scope of its work reaches beyond the original mandate. In any of these cases, the mandate group should turn the issue back to the governing bodies for resolution or request an amended mandate. In these cases it shows, while all these rules and guidelines appear mechanical in nature, it is human judgment that will determine the difference between a well-functioning organization and one that is not.

9. Executing and completing the task

It is recommended that the mandate groups hold regular meetings. It is always helpful to establish a rhythm. The committee should keep records of its proceedings, especially the key points and the results of its deliberations.

10. Evaluation

It is only after the task has been completed and the completion date has been reached that a detailed evaluation of the task and the people who performed it should be undertaken. The mandate group should be asked to do a self-evaluation and look at all aspects of their work: process and outcome. It is in the evaluation that all parties will learn the most. It is here where we can learn how to refine the process and the methodology of the mandate system for the next task. It is at this time that constructive questions can be asked why a certain course of action was taken or decision made. *An honest and constructive evaluation becomes the elixir for continuous improvement and health.* Do not sidestep this. Document the findings of the evaluation. Do not use the evaluation process as an opportunity to second-guess the final outcome or seek, in other ways, to undermine the results.

Ask yourself questions like: What worked well in terms of our task performance, reporting, and collegial relations in and outside the group? Did we have the right outside support? What would we have done differently in all these areas? In terms of the process, what recommendations can we give the governing bodies?

Above all, celebrate the accomplishments and the mistakes, the people who had the power and wisdom to delegate responsibility, and the people who were willing to assume it!

In summary,
a mandate consists of the following elements:

1. Succinct description of the task
2. Reporting responsibility
3. Decision-making authority and proposal making
4. Time line of when the task and the interim steps are to be completed
5. Membership criteria and terms of service
6. Membership selection
7. Fine-tuning the mandate
8. Process for soliciting input from constituents during the mandate
9. Executing and completing the task
10. Evaluation

Steps of a Nominating Process in a Community Meeting

1. Outline the mandate. (Remember that the mandate can be amended once the committee is functioning according to established procedures.)

2. Outline criteria for membership and the number of positions to be filled.

3. Solicit questions for clarification on the above. (In all, be brief. If major issues arise that cannot be resolved in the meeting, the governing body should be empowered to make the final call.)

4. Outline the process for selection and decision making in this meeting.

5. Solicit questions for clarification.

6. Open the floor for nominations, using the guidelines as stated above. Post the results.

7. Close the nominating process after a prearranged number of nominations if you want to place a limit on nominations. (For instance, for a group of 5 members, you may close the nominations after 6 or 7 suggestions.)

8. Have each nominee state the reasons for accepting or withdrawal.

9. Assess the end result. If you have all positions filled, you have your committee. (In some cases it may be wise to select an additional member who would function as an alternate.)

10. Before final affirmation, the selected group will have a brief conversation among themselves to consider their mandate and constellation soon after their selection, preferably before the full meeting has been adjourned. This can be done with the technique of a fishbowl (see Chapter 12, Group Exercises). This may include a brief discussion on what additional support or information they may need from the community. In some cases, an adjustment may need to be made on account of an imbalance of representation or talents. (The entire process may take around three hours to complete. Plan the meeting accordingly.)

If you have more nominees than the mandate requires, continue:

11. a. Give each person present (no absentee votes) one choice from the slate. (Nominees cannot vote for themselves but can vote for someone else.) Tabulate results. The top nominees become the committee.

    b. As in (11a) but by open ballot. (An advantage in using ballots is that participants are less swayed by comments and decisions made by those who voted before them.) The ballots and comments are read aloud once they have been collected.

    c. As in (11b) but by secret ballot. (Whenever possible, avoid this measure. Use it only when there is low trust among the members.) The facilitator, and maybe two other people who can be entrusted with this task, tabulate results and announce the nominees with the highest votes. (Ballots will be destroyed and the 3 people will commit to holding their findings in strict confidence.)

12. Re-affirm the membership by going around the circle and seek each person's final approval of the slate.

13. Debrief entire process (briefly) and share what people have learned from the process.

14. Acknowledge and celebrate accomplishments.

7

Conversation Guidelines

"What is more magnificent than Gold?" asked the King.
"Light," answered the Green Snake.
"What is more precious than Light?" he asked.
"Conversation," replied the latter.

The Green Snake and the Beautiful Lily
—Johann Wolfgang von Goethe

We commonly do not remember that it is, after all, always the first person that is speaking. I should not talk so much about myself if there were anybody else whom I know as well. Unfortunately, I am confined to this theme by the narrowness of my experience. Moreover, I, on my side, require of every writer, first or last, a simple and sincere account of his own life, and not merely, what he or she has heard of other men's lives.

from *Walden: or Life in the Woods*
—Henry David Thoreau

Bear in mind, *we cannot not communicate*! Everything we do and do not do, say and do not say conveys meaning. Studies have shown that nonverbal communication plays a much greater role in the messages that we send than anything we can verbally articulate. Our words are just the tip of the iceberg when it comes to communication. Both parties in the exchange nevertheless subliminally perceive the larger meaning of what is exchanged between the speaker and the listener. But even our words and language—mundane or profound—can carry multiple levels of meaning.

Robert Langs, in *Unconscious Communication in Everyday Life* (1993), says:

> Of all the marvels in human communication, perhaps the most awesome is the ability of the human mind to express itself simultaneously on two distinct and yet interconnected levels of meaning. And yet, this same organ can also express itself in singular, direct fashion without a trace of second meaning. Well beyond any measure of conscious control, the mind shifts automatically and almost instinctively from one form of expression to the other, depending on its own psycho-physiological state and external conditions.

Much has been made in anthroposophical and Waldorf circles of "Goethean conversation." The more intangible aspects of this methodology will come naturally to the fore when these guidelines are applied. But I hope these guidelines will give the practitioner a more detailed roadmap to the goal that all of us share: a deep, profound and effective way of communicating with, and relating to, other human beings.

These communication guidelines apply to working groups who have decision-making responsibility, especially whenever consensus is desired. Without them, consensus may appear on the surface but almost inevitably break down under the pressures of real-life situations. These guidelines are also an essential tool for open-ended conversations in large groups, as well as in a profound one-on-one conversation.

> Note: I prefer the term "guidelines" to "rules" because groups and individuals must always use their discretion in how these suggestions best fit the requirements of the moment.

At first these guidelines may appear to hinder the regular flow of a conversation rather than foster it. This is a natural phenomenon when acquiring new skills. *Before a skill is fully internalized as a part of an individual or a group, the necessary consciousness and effort required can make it awkward or even frustrating.* Have patience and perseverance.

Principle:

> Apply these guidelines when the issue or decision at hand is any one or more of the following: complex, conflicted, impacting many people (different constituencies), requiring implementation, or working by consensus. Conversely, the guidelines can be relaxed if the group is experienced and functions well or when the matter at hand is of lesser consequence.

I have a few assumptions and values that form the conceptual framework for this book.

- True communication only takes places when participants are fully transparent to each other in what they do, say, think and feel.

- The message we intended to communicate must be identical to the message received by the listener. In other words, the intention must be congruent with the result.

- An effective discussion requires that each participant is fully present and authentic, clear, specific, direct, succinct, unambiguous, speaking from his or her experience and from the heart.

• Each one of us can only be responsible for our own actions and words, not for those of others because, luckily, we have no control over other adults' conduct.

• Provided the correct methodology is used, groups can access greater wisdom and insight than the separate efforts of individuals.

1. The first guideline pertains to the seating arrangement for the group: All members of the group should be placed so that eye contact can be maintained. A circle or oval serves this purpose best. Note taking should be kept to a minimum. Minutes should be recorded toward the end of the meeting and only reflect the outcomes of the meeting. A flip chart can be used to help remind the group of important points while the meeting is in progress. The point is that no member should be burdened with constant note taking and thereby excluded from the discussion. Ideally, group members should be so engaged in the discussion as to sit on the edge of their seats for fear of missing one single word.

2. In a conversation it is very helpful to select one specific person in the group and address your comments to that person. The listener need not respond. This guideline keeps the conversation grounded in personal experience and away from abstractions. The technique is especially helpful when a conversation either overheats or loses all energy. I find that, contrary to my expectations, the rest of the group will pay closer attention to the proceeding. The opposite of this guideline confirms the wisdom of the rule: speakers addressing their comments to no one in particular will lose the attention of the group.

3. It is always helpful to briefly paraphrase the previous speaker's comments before adding your contribution. This guideline assists with the continuity and deepening of the

conversation. Paraphrasing clarifies whether the speaker has been correctly understood. You should also paraphrase when introducing a new topic. Again, this guideline can function as an inhibiter of the free flow of the conversation.

In paraphrasing a speaker must keep the following in mind:

- Paraphrase the main point only.
- Keep your paraphrase succinct and simple.
- Check with the speaker (this could be by making eye contact or orally) whether the paraphrase is basically correct. If the paraphrase is inadequate, let the original speaker make the correction and then proceed with the discussion. Others in the group may assist you with paraphrasing as long as the flow of the discussion is not compromised and you don't lose your turn to speak.
- The overall process should take a minimal amount of time unless major differences of interpretation come to light. In that case, a decision needs to be made whether the discussion should shift to deal with the differences, or remain on topic.

4. Build on the comments of previous speakers. Keep the thread of the conversation uninterrupted and alive. Avoid changing the topic until it feels just right. If you cannot connect to what the previous speaker said, hold your contribution till later. You often will find that others speak to what lives in you. This is because a well-functioning group exists within a "field" of interconnectivity.

5. *Be comfortable with silences.* These are the most precious moments in the group. It allows you to sense the greater being and wisdom that has united with the group. The conversation starts to "flow" (and everyone in the group will know it without it being verbalized) by means of active listening or speaking on the part of each member.

6. Speak only from your experience. What you hear from a third party—hearsay, in terms of experiences, perceptions or opinions—should not be part of a serious conversation in which clarity is paramount. So, too, theorizing, generalizing and hypothesizing takes away from meaningful human communication. Many of our conversations are based on these abstractions. Also, do not represent the experiences, perceptions or opinions of others. We should learn to only represent ourselves. If the contribution of someone other than those assembled is critically important to the discussion, the meeting should be adjourned and reconvened when all the necessary people can be present.

There are only two possible scenarios when speaking. (1) You can speak from your personal experience, insight, or perception. In this case, you need not authenticate your remarks by calling on the authority and support of others. (2) When appealing to the insights of other people, let them speak for themselves. I often hear the argument that others may not be in a position to speak for themselves or are unable to be present for the meeting. As adults, we need to build strength to stand up for our truth. In a genuine effort to be helpful, we can actually prevent others the empowerment and privilege to find their voices.

7. Connected with the fourth guideline, always be specific in your comments. There is no exception to this rule. Use recent and specific examples to illustrate your comments. George Sammon (a reporter with *The Washington Times*) wrote, "Specificity is the heart of credibility." I would add that specificity is a necessary condition for understanding others and for being understood.

8. Make full use of "I" statements. In the vast majority of cases, it is confusing at best—if not misleading—to use a different pronoun than the one that needs to be applied. Substituting pronouns is one of those cultural idiosyncrasies that seem to dictate that to be direct and transparent is

impolite or not sophisticated or too confrontational. The use of the pronouns, "we" or "one," instead of "I," may be acceptable in formal settings but not in group discussions.

9. Speak early in the discussion about what is important to you.

Principle:

> The more each member in a group is true to his or her insight and experience, and the earlier each member speaks to this truth, the more effectively the group will function.

Or expressed differently:

> The time and energy you spend on avoiding speaking your truth in a group, is always greater than the time and energy you spend on naming what is important to you.

Here are some examples: The room is too warm and stuffy, but no one says a word. Members repeat the same point over and over, but no one calls attention to the pattern. The discussion diverts from the agenda, and no one dares to point this out. People are restless or apathetic, but no one calls for a break. Similarly, it may be that one person is in touch with a feeling of discomfort or anger, but fails to speak to this and opts out of the discussion (maybe out of a sense of self-preservation). If a work group loses even one of its members by non-participation, the group's full potential isn't utilized.

10. Restrict your comments to one main point at a time. Observing this guideline allows the other group members to stay involved and to participate constructively. This also makes it easier for the next speaker to paraphrase your comment.

To ensure full participation on the part of all members, it may be helpful at important junctures in the discussion, to go around the circle and have each person briefly speak to the question. Another technique, used by Native American cultures, is the use of a "talking stick." Only the holder of the stick has the floor. The conversation proceeds by passing the object around in a timely fashion and to whoever seeks to be recognized.

11. Ask questions for information and clarification only. So many questions are in fact rhetorical in nature (meaning, I don't really want an answer, or the answer is implied in the question) or statements in disguise. A genuine question seeking information or an inquiry about a troubling situation is always very helpful. However, pay careful attention to how often a question is used for other than a genuine inquiry. If you have a point to make, make it without dressing it up as a question. Questions, like anything else, can either be used to obtain greater insight and connectedness, or greater distance and superficiality among the members of the group.

12. Confidentiality and disclosure: Confidentiality is often a loaded and complex issue in a group. The group should make clear at the end of its deliberations which aspects of the discussion are requested to be held in confidence. In my opinion, the only topics that qualify are those related to personnel questions and non-business agenda items, like personal sharing. Even in the case of personnel issues, your constituencies should be given appropriate updates and requests for input, as long as the lawful rights of the individual in question are not violated. The best use of the concept of confidentiality is the attitude: *I have confidence in you to*

treat what we have shared in an appropriate manner with those outside our circle. This attitude leaves people free and calls on their highest motivations.

In the vast majority of cases, the demand for confidentiality is overused and too often employed—maybe with the best of intentions—to control the legitimate flow of information to others. A good guideline to follow is the answer to the following question: *Will others be impacted in any way by our decision, or by the information we hold?* If the answer is "yes," you should disclose, and disclose early.

When in doubt, always err on the side of full and early disclosure. The tendency to hold on to and control critically important information is widespread in most sectors of our society. I have learned from difficult personal experiences that failure to disclose is poor practice and weakens the trust among those who depend on the organization and on me.

13. Connected with the above is the use of *anonymity*. In most, if not all, cases that arise in the course of daily adult interactions, anonymity is highly inappropriate. It flies in the face of being direct, honest, authentic and taking responsibility for your actions and opinions. Only in instances when physical safety is at stake (as may be the cases of abuse, or if there is a great differential of power, or when we are dealing with minors) should a person be granted anonymity.

It must be made clear to anyone who seeks some type of *action or result* from what he or she has shared in confidence, that anonymity can no longer be maintained. If a group opts to act on behalf of an anonymous person, the rest of the community is left with only partial information. This will breed distrust and lack of support.

Of course, when a person seeks anonymity, we should treat the matter with respect, understanding and diplomacy. By providing all the safeguards we can muster, we must then coach the person to a place where he or she can take responsibility for the request.

We now can summarize all of the above in the form of agreements that each one of us can make to our fellow group members. This agreement can be a formal group agreement or an informal commitment on the part of any of its members. There is, of course, no coercion placed on anyone but complete freedom to keep to the guidelines.

Group agreements

- Speak to what is important to you (thoughts, feelings, observations) in a timely manner—and in a non-accusatory, non-judgmental way.

- Be direct and specific in all your communications by using examples based on recent experiences, preferably those that transpired in the group.

- Speak from your experience only, (not from hearsay or interpretation) and therefore speak from the "I."

- As much as possible build on the comments of the previous speaker(s). This approach creates fabric of the most unexpected colors and insights.

- Paraphrase the main point made by the previous speaker. Paraphrase especially when there is emotional content, or when you seek clarity, or when you plan to change the subject.

- Honor others when they speak by letting them finish their comments.

- Ask questions only for clarification or when you need more information.

- Whenever possible, address your comments to a member in the group without expectation of a response.

- Observe silences.

- Use appropriate self-disclosure when you disclose something of a personal nature to the rest of the group.

- When necessary, disclose the assumptions and motivations that underlie your ideas, comments, and actions.

- Actively, and in a timely manner, solicit feedback from others on your behavior, comments and ideas.

- Provide feedback after being given permission from the intended recipient.

- Honor each member of the group, and leave that person free to accept or reject any or all aspects of the feedback.

- Honor requests for confidentiality, but clarify in each case that such a request is truly necessary.

- Support all group decisions as your own, whether you were present for the meeting or not.

- Be punctual by honoring meeting times.

Further process suggestions:

When in a difficult phase of a discussion, have one person speak at a time; afterward, another member of the group paraphrases what was spoken. Then proceed to the next point. You can also assign two members of the group to sit outside the circle and have them, periodically, reflect back to the group their observations and offer further process suggestions. It is extremely helpful if comments are made directly to another specific person in the group, rather than spoken abstractly into the center of the room.

8

Facilitation and Meeting Effectiveness

Facilitation is first and foremost an art. There are numerous intangibles in operation at any given time. When to intervene? When to call on a group member to finish talking? When to call on others to offer their perspectives? When to sit back and let the group do its work? When to conclude that all relevant comments have been made and call for a decision? When to call a time out and let the group reflect on what is going on? The list of options is limitless.

Luckily, there are guidelines by which a facilitator can set her compass. Other than that, it is a question of facilitating many times, as a musician practicing his instrument, to gain the necessary experience by way of trials and errors and successes.

Meetings cannot be run without good facilitation. In fact, an experienced facilitator can make the difference between a well-functioning organization, and one that is not. As the reader well knows, it is the norm and expectation for leaders in most organizations to conduct meetings for which they are responsible. This is very inefficient and ineffective, even if these leaders are capable facilitators in their own right. There is a capital rule (not just a guideline), that the facilitator should not ever be involved in the content discussion of the group. Discussing issues and conducting a meeting are two mutually exclusive activities. The reason is simply that it is nearly impossible to provide guidance on group process while at the same time holding the key to most of the relevant information, and most likely a stake in a specific outcome of the deliberations (having an agenda).

> The more facilitators get involved in the content of a discussion, the less effective their capacity to monitor and conduct group interactions.

and conversely,

> The more facilitators abstain from contributing directly to the discussion, the better they can service the group to reach the desired goals.

Leaders therefore would have to make a decision on which role to adopt. Once you have found a person who can function in the role of facilitator, leaders and the group should fully empower him/her with the mandate to run the meetings. This mandate should be established in accordance with the guidelines and procedures outlined in Chapter 6. The mandate could pertain to a single meeting or to a year-long assignment. The latter is much superior, because the role and skills of the group and the facilitator develop over time. Avoid assigning facilitators on a rotation basis. That does not help anyone.

The facilitator has a unique function and position in the organization. She should be very familiar with the issues at hand, but at the same time maintain neutrality on each of them. For some people, this is an impossible sacrifice to make. Neutrality means that any outcome, no matter whether the facilitator agrees with it or not, is supported by the facilitator. During the discussion, the facilitator's role is to inwardly step ever so slightly back from the fray so that she can keep a bird's eye view of the totality.

- The facilitator, therefore, works in unbiased and selfless service to the will of the group and the organization.

- There is a continuum at play: *the better a group functions, the less need for intervention by the facilitator.* Groups can move in and out of being effective in even one single meeting.

- *The facilitator should never expend more effort (work) than the group.* Even functions like summarizing, paraphrasing, time keeping, offering proposals, calling for a decision, etc. should as much as possible be left to members of the group. If the facilitator, at a given time, sees the need for any of these functions, she can call for it and have group members respond. It is a common occurrence for the facilitator to do all of the group's work, especially when there is low energy. When this happens, the group should stop its work—it is not productive anyway—and evaluates the causes. A shift in activity and focus (taking a brief break, playing a game, tabling the topic and moving to another) can bring the energy back into the room.

- The group and the facilitator should come to agreement prior to the meeting on what/how the group wants to be facilitated (e.g., calling on people when speaking too long or repeating themselves). In an ongoing assignment as facilitator, the agreements should be spelled out in the mandate.

The Facilitator:

- Avoids working with pre-conceived solutions.

- Acknowledges all seriously intended contributions.

- Aims to bring all members into the discussion.

- Adheres to previously agreed time frames, and contracts with the group for additional time if needed. It is my experience that more than 5 or 10 minutes overtime becomes counterproductive.

- Pays special attention to the physical surroundings and ambience of the meeting room. This includes lighting (sunlight from one angle of the room blinds those facing the light source), ambient temperature, arrangements of the tables and chairs, writing materials, prepared agendas and supporting materials, etc.

- Works together with the agenda committee and/or leadership to prepare the agenda. Days before the meeting, consults with and notifies those who present agenda items.

Note: It is unwise to hand out reading material during a discussion. You will be surprised how much this will deflate energy and scatter attention. Either hand out the supporting documents after the discussion, or beforehand and allow group members to review the document before a discussion ensues.

Meeting Effectiveness

In a healthy organization or community, there are continuous movements (information sharing loops) between the large group that provides input, guidance, support, and affirmation—and the mandate committees/individuals who do research, make proposals and decisions on behalf of the organization.

My values, beliefs and assumptions about groups:

- There will be full and egalitarian participation by all members.
- Group discussions have the potential for reaching greater insight and deeper meaning than individual research. (Of course, the one cannot happen at the exclusion of the other.)
- Decisions reached by consensus have the potential to be more successful and effective than unilateral decisions because the former have the support of everyone.
- The complexities of today's world require people to work, think, decide, and change together.
- In the Third Phase of the organization, properly mandated and organized groups are better suited to further develop and implement the vision and mission.
- Individual professional and spiritual development is no longer possible in isolation from others.
- We experience in our sleep life the perceptions and feelings that others have of us (the collective unconscious). It is therefore better to learn to articulate these perceptions to each other, than to relegate them to the collective sub-conscious of the group. Once relegated to the sub-conscious, they form and feed the greatest weaknesses and vulnerabilities of the group or organization.

I. Study

In pedagogical and other professional and service-driven organizations, it is helpful to start the meeting with a brief study or case study. I do not recommend heavy-duty reading material. I recommend a lighter study with plenty of time for all to share their experiences and thoughts. I strongly recommend an open atmosphere in which colleagues can share accomplishments, questions and problems. This is a good opportunity to further develop colleagueship, strengthen the sense of community, and foster professional learning.

II. Collegial and group development work

Do biography exercises, but make sure this is done with an agreement to not use the information gained as "evidence" to form judgments about each other. Do some form of artistic activity. Have fun. If a group or community does not have fun with their tasks, they are going down the road of complete burnout. Food is a wonderful way to enjoy the moment and build community.

III. Conducting business

There are four components to this part.

- Reports
- Discussion of issues
- Decision-making process
- Actions taken

> Note: *The important rule to observe is never to slip back and forth from one aspect of the meeting into the other.* Doing so not only alters the intent of the meeting and agenda, but each requires a different type of awareness. If a group doesn't know what will be discussed and decided and when, confusion and ineffectiveness will result.

Reports

This includes reports and updates on on-going business. It can be the most boring aspect of the meeting. It therefore is very tempting to slip into a full discussion, or to make a quick decision, just to break the monotony. In this phase, usually the first part of the meeting, people should only ask questions of clarification and be clear on next steps. Reporting should be brief and reflect the essence of the information. Find ways to make this part more interesting and engaging.

Discussion phase

There are two different types of discussion: (a) to gain greater insight on an issue or raise questions without the expectation of action or, (b) as prelude to the decision-making process. Make sure that all the relevant information is shared and available. Make sure that everyone is clear what the topic is and its aim. At the most a group can only manage an in-depth discussion on one or two items in one meeting. The purpose of a discussion is to fully explore an issue by making room for all views to be expressed. Each member should have an opportunity to share opinions/perceptions. In fact, it is unhelpful for any member to remain silent or defer to someone else to speak for him/her. Differences can stand side by side without an attempt to resolve or minimize them.

It is important that different scenarios are built in the course of the discussion. What are the alternatives? What are the different consequences of each scenario? The pros and cons? What other information is needed? Whatever you do, do not make a decision during this phase. I find that when the pressure of having to reach agreement enters, the quality of the discussion suffers.

Decision-making process

There are three modes of decision making: unilateral, consultative, and collaborative. Again, there are three distinct phases to the decision-making process: (a) defining the issue and collecting relevant information, (b) picture forming and developing different scenarios/options, (c) making the decision. The decision could include mandating a group or person to assume the task.

Week 1	Week 2	Week 3
Defining the question. Collecting all pertinent information.	Full discussion. Describing and developing alternatives & options.	Decision making using consensus model. Delegate?

Now that the group has the necessary information and has developed some possible scenarios, the group can move toward making a decision. In some case, because of the care that has been given to the first two steps, the right decision can be quite obvious. Prior to making a decision, the group should be clear whether the issue is important enough—in terms of long-term impact on the life of the organization—to require consensus. If the question is less important, it may be nice to aim for consensus, but the final decision should not be postponed if consensus cannot be reached. A mere majority or two-thirds majority agreement may suffice.

> Note: In the case of very small initiatives (around 12 to 15 people), most decisions will have to be made within the entire group. I would, however, prioritize the issues according to importance. The least important (short-term impact, affecting fewer people, etc.), should and could be mandated to individuals. The larger group may provide input (opinion, information) before the mandated person or group makes the final decision (see Chapter 6).

If the decision is complex and there are sharp differences of opinion, the group may assign a smaller group to make a preliminary recommendation. It is often helpful to have a small group (2-3 people) do the research and make a preliminary proposal. The advantage of taking this approach is that when the group continues to falter in making a decision, the sub-group can be given the responsibility (*provided the full group is clear and unequivocal in its support of the sub-group*).

> Note: Once a decision has been reached, I would strongly recommend that the decision not be undone at a later date. Too often groups make decisions only to have these amended or reversed days after they have been made. This phenomenon is extremely destructive to the life and morale of the organization. When it comes to that point, the "wrong" decision is much better than a decision that is not carried out or changed before implementation.

A decision should include not only *what* it is, but also, *who, when, how* and *where*.

Actions taken

The minute taker reads aloud all decisions that the group made in the meeting. Briefly check around to see if everyone has the same understanding (see below IV Minutes).

Review

Ask brief comparative questions: more, most, least, greatest, "golden moment," one example of what you would have done differently. What did we/you learn today?

IV. Meeting elements

Agenda setting

I recommend that two or three people take the responsibility to set the agenda in advance. The committee designs the agenda, and publishes it at least one day in advance. Items from the last meeting have already been identified. The agenda needs to be carefully designed. A judgment call would have to be made on time allotment and prioritizing the agenda items. Over the course of a week, certain issues may have arisen that need attention. But be careful not to let emergencies dominate the agenda setting. Emergencies conspire against agenda setters!

The agenda committee decides what issues require information sharing, what issues will need to be discussed, and what issues are ready for action. At the end of the previous meeting, the whole group is given a preview of the agenda for the next meeting.

The agenda includes the *order of the items, time allotted, presenter* (sponsor), and *type of discussion*.

> Note: Make it a practice to identify the person responsible for introducing the agenda item and taking responsibility for presentation of the content. As facilitator, I would still be responsible for the process. Ideally, the facilitator should not be in charge of presenting the detailed facts of a particular issue, only a rough outline of the context.

Minute taking

Minutes should be concise. It would be helpful if all groups and committees consistently held the same minute-taking format. The minutes should be brief and only reflect the essence of the discussion. Decisions/actions could be starred (***) for easy reference.

Minutes should include: (1) Date/time/place, (2) Attendance, (3) Agenda, (4) Items discussed with only "headline" descriptions, (5) A detailed description of decisions and/or actions taken, (6) Items for next week's agenda.

Time management

The group should have a timekeeper. Agree beforehand how this person is to remind the group/facilitator of the time. Realistic time slots should be assigned as part of the agenda setting. When the group goes overtime, the group "contracts" for extra time. Do this only once or twice. To add more time than the allotted time is very counter-productive.

Working with conflict, differences and power

(See Chapter 11, Conflict Management)

Transparency and confidentiality in meetings

Most of our meetings are not transparent enough. Usually a rather high wall is erected in the guise that confidentiality must be protected. It is true that in a number of instances it is important, indeed required, that meetings remain closed for purposes of maintaining confidentiality. It is also true that group members should be allowed to freely interact without having to document every word or being second-guessed. Groups have to develop a kind of "skin" in terms of their identity. The social dynamic is quite different and can be distorted when a non-member is present.

Confidentiality is required when a group or committee discusses personnel matters. Confidentiality is observed when an individual discloses personal information that is of a discretionary nature and not germane to the agenda. Only the person who discloses this information has the option to ask for confidentiality. It is no one's business to disclose personal information concerning another. Confidentiality can be maintained in any type of group development work, when business is not conducted.

All these conditions are appropriate reasons for closed meetings. However, we tend to subscribe to a silent set of norms (culture) where the first reaction is to draw the wagons in a tight circle in an effort to defend ourselves from outside critique. It is not unusual to observe groups holding on to important and relevant information for months on end, and then when a decision has been reached, the populace is notified by way of puffs of white smoke coming from the chimney.

This secluded and excluded way of working will eventually serve to alienate others from otherwise worthwhile endeavors. Transparency can be honored without compromising the necessity for confidentiality. First, all committees charged with personnel matters (hiring, firing, evaluation, remuneration, etc.) and other content-sensitive tasks (finance, tuition remission, discipline, etc.) do so under very precise mandates.

- Their mandates—including policies, procedures, and membership—are all spelled out and developed with the widest possible participation of the community on an annual basis. These mandates are consistent with the highest professional standards of practice and ethics. Therefore, when committees give periodic updates, people know what's happening.

- Secondly, all committees and governing bodies keep minutes. These minutes should reflect a skeleton record of the committee's deliberations.

- Thirdly, it is very helpful for a committee to occasionally invite others to observe one or two of its sessions and solicit their feedback, or for two committees to join forces by working on questions that affect both groups. These and other measures can foster the quality of transparency in organizations.

9

Decision-making Processes and Group Dynamics

Decisions related to the daily management of a more established institution should all be parceled out to mandate groups and individuals. The main leadership groups (Board, Director, Colleges of Teacher, etc.) should have as their main business:

- Developing and maintaining the vision and mission of an institution
- Long-term planning, long-term budgeting, and setting policies and procedures
- Mandating groups and individuals with specific tasks and responsibilities
- General development through education, training, study, art, and spiritual work
- Interfacing with, and support of, the constituents of the organization and wider community

Dino Biris (Semasea Organization Development) and Ned Hulbert et al. (Growing Edge Partners, Inc.) made a helpful distinction between three different levels of decision making: unilateral, consultative, and collaborative/consensus.

Unilateral Decision Making

The mandate holder may be either a mandate group or an individual. This level of decision making may be appropriate in any or all of the following cases:

1. The mandate holder is clearly mandated to make decisions in this area;
2. not making a decision would adversely affect operations;
3. the decision has only minor implications, and/or
4. time is of the essence.

In a great number of instances, individuals and groups working in the daily management and administration of institutions should not only be allowed but be required to make unilateral decisions for the smooth operation of the organization, as long as these decision-making powers are spelled out in the mandate.

Process:

- Whenever possible and appropriate, the mandate holder may seek prior input from colleagues and/or those most affected by the decision or those who are asked to implement it.
- The mandate holder informs all relevant parties of the decision in a clear and timely manner.
- It is the responsibility of the mandate holder to communicate in advance which decision-making mode is employed: unilateral, consultative, or collaborative.

Consultative Decision Making

It is most appropriate to use this process when:

1. The ultimate responsibility rests with the mandate holder;
2. the mandate holder needs further input,
3. the decision is of a complex or controversial nature;

4. the decision has a major effect on operations, and/or
5. has long-term ramifications.

The decision making group includes the mandate holder and all relevant parties and constituents who are affected by and/or are asked to implement the decision and/or who can contribute specific expertise.

Process:

- Constituents are identified and invited to participate.
- Nature of the decision and type of input sought is described.
- Constituents provide input and suggestions on best solution (1st input loop).
- The mandate holder makes a preliminary decision/proposal (during the meeting or after a pre-determined time) and informs the other parties.
- Constituents evaluate the preliminary decision and give further input on recommendations, if needed (2nd input loop).
- The mandate holder makes the final decision and the parties are informed of the final decision.
- If appropriate, constituents and the mandate holder convene to plan for implementation and follow-up.

> Note: Constituents must feel that their input is understood and valued. Constituents must know that the final decision may not be the one that they recommended. Whenever possible, apply the two-step input loops.

Collaborative Decision Making (working by consensus)

This mode is more easily applied in smaller groups like committees, leadership groups (Board, College, etc.). With some alterations, it can also work in large multi-constituent community meetings. It may be applied in any or all of the following cases:

1. when the decision is of a complex or controversial nature,
2. has a major effect on operations,
3. has long-term ramifications,
4. or pertains to long-term policies and procedures or visioning

Objective: The group must reach a binding decision made by consensus.

> Please note especially: The group's decision is the *final decision*. There is no higher authority or appeal. After a consensus is reached, the group must also design and implement the action phase, including who will do what and when? At the end of the process, the group reviews its work. Tasks may be delegated.

Group Dynamics

Individuals and groups make hundreds of decisions while engaged in their daily tasks. Some of these decisions pertain to the actual task at hand, while most are made on how a group chooses to proceed (process decisions). Decisions in the latter category are often made without much awareness—yet, these have the most powerful effect on task-related decisions.

1. *The group recognizes that whatever it does is what it has chosen to do. In other words, a group cannot avoid making decisions during the course of a meeting. To* not *make a decision is a decision—and one that may have many ramifications.*

In effective groups, therefore, decisions are made consciously and not by default. It is much better to decide not to make a decision than to make it by default. The group will experience decisions made by default as failures.

2. *When a group makes a decision that it does not carry out, it recognizes that the real decision was not to act.* In this case, an effective group evaluates why the apparent and the real decision were not the same.

It often happens that decisions are not implemented, or they are changed or negated only days after the apparent agreement was reached. In these cases, the group should be clear that underlying issues (usually in the realm of human relationships), or the necessary data, had not surfaced or were not fully resolved during the original discussion.

3. *The greater the number of unconscious or default decisions by a group, the more the organizational/group "shadow" is at work.* To work effectively with the unhelpful patterns in the organization, individual members of that organization must take full responsibility for their role and participation in meetings, and groups must work more consciously with decision-making processes.

It is important to remember that most decisions are not as important as they appear to be at the moment. Each decision should be taken seriously, but nothing is forever in organizational life. Many decisions are of temporal value—they have a limited "shelf life." The important point is to implement a decision and to give it time to be assimilated into the life of the organization. If it is/was a very important decision, evaluate it after a predetermined period of time. (One year is generally a good measure.)

4. *In most cases, it is better to consciously not make a decision, or even make the wrong decision, than to make a decision by default or undo a decision.* In the latter cases, the group and organization have no opportunity for learning and growing, while in the former cases we can at least extrapolate the lessons and gain new insights.

Decisions that are later retracted or changed have an enormous debilitating effect on the life of an organization. People's confidence in each other and themselves is greatly undermined when the commitment to a resolve is lacking. *The full group of people that was part of the original decision is the only one that can change a decision.*

When working in groups of over 8 to 12 members, and if a decision is of great importance, decide beforehand how the decision should be made:

- by consensus (few warrant this in-depth treatment),
- by majority vote (agree on the margin, first) or, better yet,
- by delegating it to a small group or an individual. The decision-making process should be agreed upon prior to discussing the topics. Important and complex decisions are best made over a few weeks' time.

Working by Consensus

Much has been written these days on making decisions by consensus. In academic circles, some religious movements, and many nonprofit organizations, there is a strong cultural expectation of working by consensus. There are a number of very important distinctions to consider before contemplating making a decision by consensus.

First we must be clear that, in the majority of instances, consensus decisions are not only unnecessary but can sometimes be counterproductive. Professional communities can easily be bogged down by an expectation that each decision should be made by consensus. As stated above, in the course of daily decision making, having unilateral and consultative decisions made by mandate holders is an appropriate approach. Also, I would not shy away from making decisions by majority vote, either by a 50% plus one, or a two-thirds majority, if this would break a persistent and insurmountable deadlock.

Secondly, the decision-making process can become very confusing and frustrating when the discussion on an item skips back and forth from decision-making mode to the gathering of facts, to imagining various alternative scenarios, back to decision making again. Before any group can work by consensus, it needs to carefully cultivate the correct conditions in which consensus can come to blossom. No one would expect a garden to bear fruit if the gardener did not till the soil, pull the weeds, add nutrients, and water it. So too, groups must meet all kinds of conditions before the ground is ready to productively and realistically produce decisions by consensus.

When working in very small mandate groups, consensus is pretty much the norm, as it should be. It is much easier and timesaving to resolve differences when only a few people are involved. If, after repeated attempts, consensus cannot be reached, mandate holders would need to get back to the original mandating group for further input or resolution of the issue.

Conditions prior to consensus building:

1. Always be clear—*prior to* entering the decision-making phase—how the decision is to be made: by voting (determine the margin), or consensus. Once the decision on how to

decide is made, do not deviate from that decision. In the interest of an efficient decision-making process, reserve consensus building for critically important, long-term impact issues only (see Chapter 8, Meeting Effectiveness).

2. Always make sure that all of the relevant facts have been collected and shared prior to seeking consensus. Never ignore this important second step. Groups often stumble over this elementary requirement. The group and facilitator should ask themselves, do we have all the information necessary to make a decision by consensus?

3. Always make sure that the various options and alternatives have been fully explored and described before seeking consensus. Do not by-pass this important third step. Each agenda item for discussion invariably has multiple options as possible solutions. The group must fully develop each option. Describe the pros and cons involved. Weigh the possible impact—positive and negative—that each of these options may bring. Suspend the temptation to quickly come to a judgment. This way, the group has a full spectrum of possible solutions in front of it, so that its members can make informed decisions. The more time is spent on this phase of the discussion, the easier it is to reach consensus afterwards.

4. In addition to these conditions, all the guidelines outlined in chapter 7 (Conversation Guidelines) are absolutely integral to this methodology.

Even if these conditions are met, groups tend to just embark on the discussion in the hope that by massaging the question back and forth, consensus will eventually arise by responding to individuals' contributions until their concerns have been satisfactorily addressed.

Caroline Estes (1983) has made helpful suggestions on the process and the role that group members play in reaching consensus. For instance, she makes a distinction for those who oppose a particular decision to either "stand aside" (to allow the majority opinion to prevail) or to "block" it, which means the decision is effectively vetoed. The Quaker tradition, too, has a great and very valuable approach to reaching consensus—one steeped in a rich spiritual practice (Morley 1993). In addition, there is a very particular methodology that will virtually ensure a transparent (if secular) and replicable process.

The greatest dilemma for groups seeking to work by consensus is: what to do when a small minority opposes the consensus, even after an in-depth discussion and a clearly defined process? What is the norm by which the group wants to operate? Some groups would insist on a true consensus, which means that anyone can hold veto power over the majority. Conversely, if the group can tolerate proceeding with the decision in spite of minority dissent, it decides by majority rule. Groups should answer these questions for themselves before they embark on making decisions. There are also certain techniques like taking a time-out by tabling the decision, or empowering a subgroup to make the decision on behalf of the full group (see Chapter 6, The Mandate System).

There are five elements that stand central to this methodology:

- The group adheres to the conversation guidelines as described in Chapter 7.
- The role and function of the facilitator is as described in Chapter 8.
- There are both discussion and written components in this process.
- Each group member takes an integral and active role in each phase of the process. No one can hide from the process, or dominate it.
- At various points, the full group divides into much smaller groups, and there are solo tasks for individual members.

Consensus Building Process (Short version)

This version, or a variation thereof, is used when the question at hand is relatively simple, straightforward and one-dimensional.

1. The group has determined that consensus is desired and that the above-mentioned conditions have all been met.

2. The question for consideration is clearly stated and posted. There can be no ambiguity about the task. (5 minutes)

3. A brief time is taken for each individual member to reflect and write down his or her thoughts. The reason for this step is to have members clearly identify their preferences without the push and pull of hearing others express their opinions. (5 minutes)

4. The full group convenes and all members are asked to share their opinions. It is important that everybody speak. The facilitator makes sure that comments are brief and to the point. If a particular contribution is unclear, the speaker should be asked to clarify, and others may help by paraphrasing. (15 minutes)

5. Once everyone is heard, commonalities and differences are noted (on flipcharts if necessary). The pulse of the meeting is taken by asking people if the group is close to consensus or not. (10 minutes)

6. If it appears that with some small adjustments full consensus can be reached, the question can be formulated and called. *However*, even if consensus appears possible, each and every member speaks to the question and articulates why he or she supports the decision. In this way, a much greater clarity is reached and therefore there is a much higher level of

commitment to the decision. This method also holds people much more accountable for their decision, because they cannot afterwards (because of their silence) claim that consensus was not reached with their full support. (10–15 minutes)

If great differences remain—rather than asking individuals to step aside to allow for consensus—the conversation continues by describing the differences and exploring the objections and reservations on a deeper level than before. *It is always surprising to see how much agreement can be reached once people know their point of view was taken seriously and taken into consideration.*

Consensus Building Process (Full version)

This version, or a variation thereof, is used when the question at hand is more complex, having multiple components requiring a full written statement (such as a vision statement), instead of just a "yes" or "no" in answer to a question.

1. The group has determined that consensus is desired.

2. The question for consideration is clearly stated and posted. There can be no ambiguity about the task. (5–10 minutes)

3. A brief time is taken for each individual member to reflect and write down his or her thoughts. (5 minutes)

4. Small groups of 4 to 8 members are formed to share and discuss the individual findings. People contribute from what they have written down. A discussion follows to identify similarities and differences. From this discussion, the groups are asked to draft a preliminary (brief) statement in response to the question. Each group does the same. (20–25 minutes)

5. The full group posts all draft statements and briefly solicits individual comments on the results. Typical observations

pertain to general trends, commonalities and differences. At this point, it is rare to get comments from individuals that their views are not represented, or that some people feel their opinions are not heard. That is because, (a) everyone contributed to the draft process, and (b) if one group did not reflect a particular point of view, surely other groups did. (10–15 minutes)

6. Step 4 is repeated, but this time Group A takes the existing statement from Group B, Group B the statement from Group C, and so on. The instruction to each group is that they may only refine and modify, but not add major components to the statements. They have to write within the framework provided. (20 min) This process ensures that everyone can take ownership of what is written without anyone taking *sole* ownership. It now truly belongs to the entire group. Taking ownership this way is not a theoretical possibility; it is an actual experience.

7. Again, the full group gathers for people to offer general comments, identify trends and differences, and glaring omissions. Observations are solicited to see if the group feels they are getting closer to the desired results. Another iteration of steps 6 and 7 may have to be required, but in most cases this is not necessary. (15 minutes)

8. As the next-to-last step, a small writing committee of 2–3 people is formed—people who have the ability to see the larger trends in the statements and who have writing/editing skills—to draft a brief statement reflecting the total input of all who participated in the process. (15–25 minutes) The rest of the group takes a break or attends to other business.

9. The final product is presented to the full gathering for review. At this point there may be some minor changes suggested, if necessary. Any last minute fine-tuning takes place with all present. (10 minutes)

10. Going around the circle, *each* member of the group affirms orally his or her support of the document. Once that is done, people are invited to share some brief observations about the process. (15 minutes) The group has now come to a true and unanimous consensus decision.

10

Community Vision Building and Planning by Consensus

Here is a vision-building process, based on true consensus, which can be conducted in large and diverse groups and communities, as well as in smaller groups. Marvin Weisbord and many other associates originally developed this technique. There are many different variations of this methodology conditioned by the situation and circumstances. This process can also be used to resolve long-standing conflicts among different constituencies and cultures. The following is a rendition and approximate adaptation of a *Future Search Conference* methodology (Emery 1993, 1996) and *Future Search* (Weisbord 1992, 2000).

Conceptual Framework and Core Values

- The first assumption is that people can understand the world in which we live, and therefore also the organizations and institutions we have created. And since the world is knowable, people can make rational decisions to make the changes they seek.
- When given the chance, people are eager to be fully engaged with all their capacities and to make a positive contribution to the institutions of which they are members.
- Creating a better future should not be the exclusive province of the elite.
- Everyone is of equal importance, in spite of the different functions each may perform in the organization.

- Diversity should not only be appreciated, but also actively sought.
- Bring all stakeholders into the room.
- Possibilities matter more than perceived limitations.
- The universe receives any organization, with its strengths and weaknesses, problems and gifts.
- *Consensus is valid only to the extent to which each individual asserts his/her own relation to the facts and retains his/her individuality; there can be no genuine agreement, unless each adheres to the testimony of his or her experience and steadfastly maintains a hold on reality.*

Margaret Wheatley's explorations of the New Science—chaos theory in physics, the self-organizing properties of information as a natural process—suggest a hypothesis:

> That is that these meetings engage not only our heads but our hearts, guts, and unconscious "data" in very powerful and potentially valuable ways. They can also be at times scary, leading to feelings that we are "out of control." That concern, I believe, is the single biggest reason leaders may hesitate to take this path of future search conferencing.

Our experience in using Future Search Conference in organization and community development indicates that a two-to-five-year period is realistic for substantial changes. The Search concept is based on two assumptions about the present state of social change:

1. Accelerated rates of change on all levels of society have created what Emery and Trist (1960) called "turbulent environments." Turbulence means that an organization's context has become unstable and more unpredictable.

2. An organization in a turbulent environment faces problems not clearly defined or understood by conventional methods. Thus the right methods or solutions are not known. The organization must search for new forms of functioning or, in evolutionary terms, adapt to environmental changes by creating new behavior. We call this a search process since a form of learning through trial and error takes place.

According to David Bohm (1991), we should create situations where we can suspend our opinions and judgments in order to listen to each other. The idea is that we might generate a kind of social superconductivity by having lots of energy in the exchange, while keeping the temperature low (as in physics). It later became clear to him that, no matter what we do in science or in any other area,

> ...it will not help if we don't find a way to be related to each other at a deeper level. And, any group organized around a leader, ideology, theory, or agenda creates a group identity that inevitably brings it into conflict with other groups and individuals.

The sad but obvious fact is that even organized groups with the highest ideals end up adding to the general cacophony of organized groups vying to solve the world's problems. But what would happen if 20 or 30 people—who had in common only an uneasiness over the current state of humankind—simply met to attempt a dialogue?

And Roger Harrison (1983) adds:

> We can take the view that our organization has an appropriate place in the larger systems, and that our task as management and leaders is to attune our organization to our environment . . . to discover what our part is and play it. . . . From a systems point of view, then, strategic thinking is a search for meaning, rather than for advantage.

From systems theory, we know that each organization evolves in relationship to a larger whole and that closed or isolated systems cannot change and grow.

Essential components and principles

The general flow of the conference leads from the present → to the past conditions and history of the organization → to an ideal future envisioned → back to the present → to planning and implementation of the vision → to evaluation, review and celebration.

There is a continuous movement back and forth between smaller groups and the full community throughout the three-day event. Smaller groups are tasked to explore and research specific questions, and the entire community convenes to share the results and provide further input and feedback. This movement back and forth mirrors the expansion and contraction phases in all living organisms.

At critical points when a clearly articulated statement is required, a small sub-group can be formed to "wordsmith" the results of the entire group. This sub-group has heard all the input and deliberations. Its final statement should be succinct but include all the aspects of the desired statement. Furthermore, the final statement must be approved by each and every participant in the room for it to become an official document.

Phase 1. World trends (Desirable/Probable)

The first phase accomplishes (1) the creation of a shared context, (2) the expression of values in the context, and (3) the realization of collective action and decision making as group. To ensure a vision that truly reflects the values and hopes of those assembled, the findings and recommendations of one group are handed to the next group for further development.

This is done with each sub-group. Each session is not much more than 30 minutes in duration. Doing it this way ensures a thorough, in-depth yet realistic, egalitarian process. These steps can be repeated once or twice or even more times. Between the steps, the full group assembles briefly to get a sense of the totality, then sub-groups continue their work.

Phase 2. Trends that affect the organization (Desirable/Probable)

The second phase is characterized by more detailed description and knowledge that correspond to defining the operating environment of the system (organization).

Phase 3. Evolution of the organization

In the third phase attention is drawn to the evolution (biography) of the system—its strengths and weaknesses—and a time line of the main events in its history.

Phase 4. The future of the organization (Desirable/Probable)

This phase explicitly calls for creativity and innovation. The future of the system can now be designed using ideal characteristics and *not* directed toward concrete strategies or solutions, but, rather, we suggest that people devise *curative, unconventional, and surprising* conceptions of what the system ought to be. When a small group generates enough information, it exchanges its work with that of another group. By introducing stakeholder scrutiny, ideas that would be supported quickly emerge, and those who have selected the ideas are more likely to be committed to implementation strategies. Finally, the work of each group is merged through a discussion of differences and similarities, and a consensus scenario is created.

Phase 5. Strategies

The formation of strategies follows the same mode as the previous phase. Small groups generate the means by which the idealized future can be obtained and develop a list of strategies that the group endorses. A copy of this document is supplied to each group. Creative ways of bringing about the desired future are produced in the brainstorming mode. Small groups do the sorting out of all the suggested strategies. Once the strategies are articulated, participants then self-select action planning groups to design implementation plans for their chosen strategies. The products of the action groups are presented to the large group for discussion of their desirability and feasibility. It works much better to send the same work groups back to consider the viability of their implementation plans, given the contextual and operating environment trends that they have identified. earlier Finally, participants are asked how they will integrate the plans in their day-to-day operations when they return to work the following day. A mutually agreed follow-up program provides a tracking system for the whole group.

Ground rules:

- Members of horizontal groups (functional groups) do not need to agree among themselves. The purpose is to generate as many ideas as possible.
- Heterogeneous groups (cross-functional groups) are asked to find agreement, the common ground on which we stand.

- All members have an equal chance to express views.
- At the stage of exploration and brainstorming, there is no problem solving. Learning, awareness, understanding, and mutual support will be the focus.
- Every idea and comment is valid. People need not agree.
- All items are flip-charted to make it "common property" of the entire group.
- The group will honor time commitments.
- No lectures.
- Facilitators structure tasks and manage time.
- Participants generate and analyze information, drive meanings, propose action, and take responsibility for the output.

The following guidelines are used:

- Forming categories: Predicted changes can be arranged into a limited number of categories or headings, preferably not to extend for longer than 5-6 years.
- Identifying boundaries beyond local control: Many external changes will occur. It is possible, however, to meet such trends with an active, adaptive strategy.
- Differences in perspective are not necessarily disagreements. Views can be complementary and can comprise common ground for further discussion.
- The social environment may appear contradictory and so complicated that the capacity for action is impaired. Contradictions can be clarified and complexity reduced.

- Conflict of interest can be made explicit. This can form the basis, not for getting rid of conflicts, but for agreement about how to handle them.
- Problems can be redefined in operational terms and in ways that allow for open discussion.
- Predictions and forecasts may be wrong. Future Search Conference predictions, however, do provide valuable information about how people perceive the present, which then can serve as a basis for further discussion. The main purpose of these steps is to identify common ground for action.
- Plans for action: In this process, the first step is to identify problems and then suggest possible remedies. Sub-groups are self-selected by areas of interest. Finally, groups present integrated plans with priorities on short- and long-term actions and discuss these in plenum. Project groups may form and take responsibility for later implementation.

Long-term Planning

Definitions

- *Vision Statement*: The vision is a clear statement of "where we want to go and/or be in the future." The vision is an existential declaration. It is the star that guides all our actions and sets a direction. The vision statement is a succinct declaration of the purpose and identity of the organization. A vision is like that powerful speech by Dr. Martin Luther King, "I have a dream..."

- *Mission Statement:* The mission statement is a course of action by which we will achieve our vision and the values and assumptions supporting it. It is a broad statement of the unique functions the organization performs. Examples: "We will achieve our vision by being customer-focused." Or, "Every child will receive an education that is tailored to his or her specific needs and capabilities."
- *Objectives:* Objectives are long-term goals and pertain to what we do and how we do it—what we hope to achieve.
- *Goals:* Short-term objectives: measurable, obtainable, here-and-now, specific.
- *Strategies:* The actions we will take to accomplish the above—how we will accomplish what we want to do.
- *Structures:* All the systems and policies that need to be in place to accomplish our goals.

At the end of a long-term planning conference, there will be a vision that is workable and energizing for the entire group of stakeholders. There will also be specific action plans for the entire organization, for sub-groups (functional and cross-functional), as well as individual commitments and action plans for the immediate future—starting today! The vision and mission statements and each element of the plan are approved by consensus of all participants.

Schedule for a Typical Planning Event

DAY ONE

- Welcome
- Purpose and overview of the conference
- Introduction of all participants (could be done as a brief exercise or game)
- Working guidelines of conduct and communication. Set of agreements among participants (time management, etc.)
- Explanation/demonstration of and agreement to decision-making modes

Trends

1. (In small groups) Describe trends that appear to affect our lives (politics, economics, technology, religion, nature, demographics, world and local events, family, education, life-style, workplace environment). Each group identifies 3 main trends.

2. (Full group) Share findings and briefly note similarities and differences.

3. (Small groups) Identify trends that appear to affect our organization in general (human/material resources, human relations, local/national/international markets, nature, employment, clients, quality/standards, finance, politics, safety, ergonomics, education).

4. (Full group) Share findings and briefly note similarities and differences.

5. (Small groups) Determine which of those trends we can affect (to some degree) and those that are beyond our control. Each group identifies 3 main trends in each category.

6. (Full group) Share findings and briefly note similarities and differences.

7. (Full group) Movement/game/problem-solving activity to energize, have fun and learn.

Biography

1. (Full group) Construct a brief history (biography) of the organization and time line of main events (milestones) of the organization, concentrating on the early days, vision and intentions.

2. (Fishbowl) A small group identifies a couple of main themes and patterns in the center of the large group (the fishbowl technique is described in Chapter 12). Afterwards the large group provides further observations and experiences. Record results on a flipchart.

3. (Small groups) Identify 2 or 3 accomplishments and shortcomings/failures in the life of the organization.

4. (Full group) Share findings and briefly note similarities and differences. Group celebrates accomplishments, and acknowledges shortcomings.

Predictions

1. (New small groups) Identify and specify trends likely to affect the organization over the next 2-5 years. (Refer to the findings above under Trends.)

2. (Full group) Share findings and briefly note similarities and differences.

3. (Small groups) Determine which of those trends we can affect and those that are beyond our control. Each group identifies only 3 main trends in each category.

4. (Full group) Share findings and briefly note similarities and differences.

5. (Full group) Identify future trends—those we can affect and those we cannot.

6. (Full group) Share general insights. Brief review and closing words. Perhaps a story?

DAY TWO

- Full group check-in. No more than 10 minutes. Only brief impressions and new insight are solicited.
- Overview of the day ahead.
- Brief presentation if appropriate.

Visioning

1. (Individual) Write, or in pairs discuss, a fictional newspaper article written 2–5 years from now.

2. (Cross-functional groups) Each person shares a blue-sky future scenario with the others—services, products, markets, values, vision, dreams, compensation, benefits, public image, professional relationships, employees, practices, policies, work environment and processes, etc. (It is a given that each group cannot cover all areas, but once the full group convenes, a complete picture will arise.) Each group share its finding in the full group. At this point, there are no comments, only questions for clarification.

3. Pass results/findings from each group to the next group. This group will build on and/or refine results, but cannot introduce new items. Must eliminate and/or combine

scenarios. Group has to *agree* on 1 or 2 scenarios for presentation. Likely trends, as identified yesterday, are considered.

4. (Marketplace) Results are posted around the room and one person represents the group. Everyone else mills around and briefly comments or asks a question from the reps. Input is written down on the flipcharts.

5. Back in the small group, input is duly considered and the group has to agree on the final draft of its scenario for presentation. Results are posted for everyone to see.

Planning

1. In a fishbowl, representatives from each sub-group identify strategies for consideration for these futures (such as, developing a vision statement, list of core values, new product development, marketing plans, networking with other organizations and services). The large group provides input. The fishbowl group must then agree to a final list of topics that require detailed planning.

2. By self-selection, individuals consider and commit to a topic for which they will develop an implementation plan.

3. These groups then develop a specific action plan (desired outcome) that incorporates: *what* (be clear about the topic and what they want), *who* (who should be part of this now and/or in the future), *how* (decisions to be made, to whom they report, procedures, etc.), *where*, and *when* (time line).

4. Each group must come to consensus on the plan and present this to the large group for their final input.

5. Incorporating this input, each group presents the final draft of its proposals.

Final Plenum and Commitments

- Share and celebrate results
- Individual commitments to the plans
- Next steps
- Review
- Closing remarks

11

Conflict Management

Conflict is an integral and important part of all social interactions, whether this is in a group setting or just between two individuals. Nonprofit organizations based on spiritual values and ideology are not immune to this fact. We may often have the experience that conflicts find their way into these communities with particular intensity and persistence.

In working with conflict and trying to resolve it, we must be clear that there are no proven models or easy steps to follow. Each situation is unique and demands our full attention and awareness so that we may come to an appropriate response. Today we are asked to create a new understanding and reach binding agreements, what in earlier times may have been prescribed by established cultural norms or institutional authority. Often we may not know if our actions and solutions are correct for a given situation until we have tried, even experimentally, and then consciously evaluated the results.

This chapter explores aspects of the nature of conflict and the role it plays within the structure and development of social life. We will examine our own relationship to conflict and offer possible guidelines and techniques on working with conflict.

> The absence of conflict does not necessarily mean there is harmony; more likely it may mean apathy.

Dimensions of Conflict:

- *The chance for a conflict to escalate is greater when we ignore or avoid the conflict.*
- *The more we are emotionally or materially dependent on another person or persons, the greater the chance for conflict.* In other words, conflict usually occurs within the context of interdependency.
- Two people in conflict often share those negative character traits that they perceive and then proceed to criticize in the other. It is somewhat ironic that I will seek to find those people who best represent character traits that I am determined to avoid seeing in myself.
- Differences become conflicts when they are accompanied by emotions. Concepts and ideas do not create conflict. In my experience, strongly expressed intellectual arguments are often thinly disguised but potent emotions. Fear of the unknown and loss of control are possibly the greatest sources for creating and maintaining conflict.
- Another interesting fact is that conflict provides for greater energy in the group. Intellectual processes, while necessary, tend to lessen the energy in the group and inhibit creativity.

The Role of Conflict

In the unfolding of a meeting, all of us can confirm the experience when, after a difficult moment—going through "the eye of the needle" by means of a confrontation—the meeting can reach a deeper level of significance. Once that happens, everyone knows it and is inspired by it. The meeting becomes more efficient without losing the necessary depth of deliberation.

To recognize, allow for, and process the expression of conflict and differences among members of a group has many benefits. It provides a healthy diversity that will energize all members of a group. It allows for much greater individual and group learning and growth. Working groups will gain greater flexibility and adaptability to meet the ever-increasing demands placed on organizations. Through our differences, a more meaningful unity and connection can arise with a sense of purpose. Individual contributions, pertaining to the life and performance of the group are recognized as being essential to the success of the whole group.

Without conflicts, we would fall into blissful but dulling sleep. Among other things, conflict awakens us. Some communities appear to be addicted to conflict. Maybe it is because people intuitively sense that conflict raises consciousness. Or it may be that staying in conflict enables the community to avoid working on other, more controversial, issues.

If conflict awakens us, we may extrapolate that the more conscious we are as human beings, the fewer instances of conflict are experienced as negative. In other words, we still recognize the difficulties in life, but they are experienced as opportunities and used to make progress. When we view it as a life-long process, we slowly gain a different relationship to what we used to call conflict.

The following letter was written by Fra Giovanni Giocondo to his friend, Countess Allagia Aldobrandeschi on Christmas Eve, 1513.

> I am your friend and my love for you goes deep. There is nothing I can give you which you have not got, but there is much, very much, that, while I cannot give it, you can take.
>
> No heaven can come to us unless our hearts find rest in today. Take heaven!

No peace lies in the future which is not hidden in this present little instant. Take peace!

The gloom of the world is but a shadow. Behind it, yet within our reach is joy. There is radiance and glory in the darkness could we but see—and to see we have only to look. I beseech you to look!

Life is so generous a giver, but we, judging its gifts by the covering, cast them away as ugly, or heavy or hard. Remove the covering and you will find beneath it a living splendor, woven of love, by wisdom, with power.

Welcome it, grasp it, touch the angel's hand that brings it to you. Everything we call a trial, a sorrow, or a duty, believe me, that angel's hand is there, the gift is there, and the wonder of an overshadowing presence. Our joys, too, be not content with them as joys. They, too, conceal diviner gifts.

Life is so full of meaning and purpose, so full of beauty—beneath its covering—that you will find earth but cloaks your heaven.

Courage, then, to claim it, that is all. But courage you have, and the knowledge that we are all pilgrims together, wending through unknown country, home.

And so, at this time, I greet you. Not quite as the world sends greetings, but with profound esteem and with the prayer that for you now and forever, the day breaks, and the shadows flee away.

Elements of Conflict Resolution

The following elements are listed, but not placed in order of priority or importance. They should all live in our consciousness as we work with conflict.

Inner mobility of thought

There cannot really be a question of fully resolving a conflict. Some elements in conflict dissolve naturally, while others may lead to the next level of challenges in the future. The first element in approaching conflict resolution is to unlock a situation so that movement can be brought into fixed perceptions that people have of each other and of issues, if only for a brief moment. Changing our perceptions means the parties learn to see the situation from the opposing point of view ("to walk in the other's shoes"), so that they gain greater empathy and understanding for the other. If this movement can take place, conflict becomes a dynamic force for change and development.

Respecting the process

The second element in conflict resolution is to use a process that allows the necessary learning and skill building to occur. How we go about resolving a conflict is as important as the resolution itself. Conflict, after all, often arises because of a breakdown of due process. Here are some examples of process questions:

- Are all the people who are affected by the conflict part of its resolution?
- Is there enough safety provided by means of adequate listening and communication techniques?
- Is there enough safety provided by means of a prior agreement not to shame and blame each other?

- Is there enough safety provided by means of neutrality of space and neutrality of the person who facilitates the discussion?
- Are the objectives of the meeting clear?

It is a misconception to think that appropriate conflict resolution means that the parties live happily ever after. The most important purpose of our work must be that paralyzing conflict can turn into creative difference and constructive diversity in our organizations. Without diversity, our organizations and human relationships turn stale and stagnant.

Cultivating trust

Trust is probably the main element necessary for resolving differences. The dilemma is that in most, if not all cases, trust has seriously eroded between the parties. Rebuilding trust does not happen by asking for it or, even worse, demanding it. *Trust can only be rebuilt in small and obtainable steps. It is gradually rebuilt from positive experiences.* For instance, parties may reach agreement on a couple of minor issues, or they may perform a small task that is of interest to both. Or, they may agree to some minor behavioral changes in how they interact with each other. Whatever it is, it must be achievable, measurable and lead to success.

As soon as progress is made in building trust and the parties sense that there is improvement, it may be very tempting to think that now we have resolved the conflict. Often this is not the case. Because the emotional and material costs can be so high, parties have an interest in declaring early victory.

Narration

We now need to turn to some of the facts surrounding the situation. One of the most effective elements in resolving conflict is that the conflict must be articulated and fully described. In other words, the conflict must become perceptible: perceptible—not only in its effects (because, most likely, the effects are painfully clear to all)—but we must learn to describe the essential facts and circumstances and chronology of the conflict. It is like storytelling. Many may find this a difficult moment and arduous process, but taking this step will have a very important benefit. By describing what was hidden, we externalize and thereby objectify the difficulties. Invariably, overlooked and simple facts are discovered that shed new light on the whole situation. With this, the conflict loses its destructive grip on the parties. The exercise alone of narrating the conflict has a liberating effect.

Commitment to seek a resolution

The fifth element is to have the will to find a solution! While conflict can inflict great misery on all parties (sometimes for long periods of time), people may still be reluctant to seek a resolution. There can be many reasons for this reluctance. Resolution brings with it the necessity for change and for more work on the part of all members in a group and more accountability to oneself and others. It may, therefore, feel safer and more convenient to stay with the status quo of existing power structures.

When asked to facilitate conflict resolution, it is very important to assess how committed the parties are to finding a resolution. There are various ways to assess this commitment. We must pay attention to what people say or more importantly, pay attention to their actions. What is the mood in a meeting? How genuine is the level of exchange? How willing are the parties to commit to extra meeting time and to allot the necessary material and human resources to the process? Do people show up late for meetings? Do they "forget" important agreements? Does another conflict suddenly take precedence? On a subconscious or deliberate level, individuals and groups can be ingenious in avoiding dealing with the issues at hand.

Courage to face one's shadow side

Intimately connected with the commitment to find a resolution, is the element of courage. In working with conflict we inevitably are confronted, not only with the shadow side of the other person, but also with that of ourselves. It takes real fortitude to face one's demons, especially in a public or semi-public setting. But we must ultimately be able to do so if we consider ourselves to be in service to the organization and its mission. After all, we all joined the various service institutions, and even businesses, because we believed in the cause. In the vast scheme of things, what would we be willing to abandon: the causes for which we were willing to fight, or our sense of self-righteousness?

Tolerance

Few of us can say that what we perceive as shortcomings in the other cannot be found in ourselves. A precondition for working with conflict is that we don't place ourselves above the others in the conflict. Any sentiments that make us feel that another person's problem couldn't be our own, works against the process of resolution. Honest and heart-felt humility joined by a certain fearlessness are all essential ingredients.

A nonjudgmental attitude must pervade all that we do. We must not find fault with a person or try to find one party right or wrong in a situation. Everyone involved in the conflict has contributed to the conflict. By taking sides or pronouncing opinions and explanations, we only add fuel to the conflict. We should be very careful to distinguish the processes of conflict resolution from those of evaluation. The latter aims for a decision or corrective action of some sort. The former is purely designed to accommodate communication and further development.

Respecting our freedom

We must respect the freedom of the other human being to act or not to act in any aspect of the resolution process. If we recognize that each conflict finds its origin within the souls of the individual parties to the conflict, then resolution must start with accepting our own responsibility in the conflict. We must know that no matter how obvious the shortcomings of the other may be, or how radically wrong his thinking is, I have only the power to change myself. *No amount of effort on my part can make me change the other person or have him learn the lessons that I think life is teaching him.* The idea of honoring the unequivocal freedom of the other human being to participate on any level of the process must permeate all our feelings and actions.

Authenticity

There are three additional elements that are important to remember and to apply whenever we can. One is that when we are speaking—of human interaction, colleagueship, and especially in difficult relationships—it is important that we learn to speak authentically from our truth and personal perspectives. It is a mystery that as adults we are so awkward and suspicious of expressing our true experiences with each other. In our frailty and striving we bear witness to our humanity. The more real we are to each other, the less conflicted our differences. Truth spoken in a non-threatening way, is both disarming and refreshing.

Emphasize the future

Never mind our differences and varied backgrounds; common ground can always be found when parties agree on future behaviors and develop future goals. It is unrealistic and unnecessary to spend precious resources and human capital on reaching agreement on past incidents or present conditions. We cannot change what was, only what we want to create together.

Systems thinking

The last element concerns group work. In the vast majority of cases, a conflict between two members of a working group will adversely affect the working of the entire group. This particular conflict will live in the consciousness of, and becomes the burden of, the whole group. Additionally, almost without exception, other members of the group will find their alliances to the conflict and subsequently contribute to it. For these reasons, *resolution should always take place within the context of the full group.* The benefit to this approach is simply that other members can become co-responsible for the process and, when resolution occurs, share the benefits and sense of accomplishment. Please resist the temptation to have conflicts resolved outside the circle of people who are affected by the conflict. In many work communities, there is still a strong tendency to view conflict as dirty laundry that should be washed in private. But rather than seeing conflict as dirty laundry, we should regard it as a weed in a community garden, for which all of us are responsible and all reap the benefit when it is cleared.

Summary

- Embrace and accept conflict; do not see it as extraneous to life or as an unavoidable evil.
- "Unfreeze" the opinionated perceptions we carry of others, the issues and ourselves.
- Trust is a key ingredient to resolving conflict. Trust, however, does not appear of its own accord. It can only be established or re-established in small steps made by both parties.
- Make conflict perceptible. Once a conflict is named and fully articulated in terms of the main issues and chronology of events, the group has a realistic chance to work effectively with the conflict.
- Parties must have a true commitment to resolving the conflict. Don't just listen to what people say, but also assess their willingness to allocate precious time

and other resources, and their ability to keep to agreements.

- A willingness to work with conflict takes courage by all parties. Resolving conflict often means a departure from the comfortable status quo by entering uncharted territories. Professional relationships may have to be re-defined, new obligations undertaken, and/or organizational structures redesigned. The feeling of uncertainty often accompanies communities that have a willingness to experiment with new ideas and social forms as part of processing conflicted situations. The collective maturity if a community is commensurate with how much it can tolerate uncertainty and paradox.
- Be nonjudgmental to an extreme! Judgments only beget more judgments. Opinions beget more opinions. Who is willing to break this cycle of an "eye-for-an-eye"? There is of course a vital role for making discerning judgments and evaluations. But this comes at the conclusion of a fully executed process of conflict resolution, not prior to or during to it.
- Honor the freedom of each fellow human being to do the work that he or she needs to do in his or her time. Only in the most extreme circumstances will this principle interfere with the healthy running of an organization.
- Never assign the fault of a difficult situation to one person or group. In human relationships, causality is circular. Any attempt to work back to the source or cause of a conflict will lead you to discover yet another condition that preceded it—ad infinitum.
- Speak from your heart and be authentic in all your communications.
- Resolve conflicts within the full circle of human beings are affected by, and contribute to, the conflict.

Steps

This outline of steps in conflict resolution is much more a general guide than a rigid formula. When we facilitate or directly engage in confronting a conflict, our intuitions will guide us through the process. Very often individual steps may have to be bypassed, or it may be sufficient to just cover a couple of these "check points." To better illustrate these steps, we will assume that the conflict has escalated substantially, affecting various individuals and different segments of the organization.

1. Assessment and Commitment Phase

This first stage is significant because it will lay a foundation and set a tone for the entire process. Primarily, we are considering three interrelated steps. First, there must be an acknowledgment and identification of the problem or conflict by all the parties involved. Everyone is usually aware of the problem and the urgent need for finding a working solution.

Second, some kind of assessment is made about how the problem should be resolved. Decisions are made on how to approach the difficulties. It may just be that two individuals should get together and talk it out, or that existing channels of communication and/or procedures should be followed; or it may be decided that a third party be brought in (from inside, or outside the organization's community) to facilitate the process.

Third, whatever the decision is, the main parties to the conflict must understand, agree, and commit to the process. Without some basic agreement among the parties, resolving a conflict is practically impossible. In the latter case, a community might find itself making an evaluative decision to create an arrangement that will allow for the continued running of the organization. These decisions may run from binding arbitration to a negotiated settlement, probation, or asking an individual to resign. Any of these responses may be legitimate and necessary in certain cases, but it should be remembered that a conflict could easily metamorphose and shift to other areas and individuals in the organization's community, once the identified problematic individual leaves.

2. Biographical and Descriptive Phase

As mentioned earlier, this phase is crucial. When special care has been exercised to make the conflict fully perceptible, a resolution may appear. In this phase, therefore, it is our aim to fully articulate what the conflict is and sketch its history. We map the conflict. While it is important to achieve clarity in describing the circumstances, do not overload it with minute details but learn to characterize the essence of the conflict. Sometimes this can even be done with an image. In this process, it will become clear where the story coincides with people's perceptions and memory and where it does not.

If individuals strongly disagree on the course of events and nature of the conflict, we let these discrepancies stand. These discrepancies are part of the complexity of the conflict. Furthermore, at this stage we concentrate on bringing problems to light, not on solving them. It is a very necessary, though painful, moment in the process to have all parties experience the severity of the conflict.

3. Perception Sharing and Mirroring Phase

This phase is truly the heart of the resolution process. Following and interlocking with phase two, phase three focuses on the actual interrelationships between people in the conflict. What are the perceptions that others hold of me? What is the impact of my behavior on others? Are my actions consistent with my intentions? Is what I say consistent with what I truly feel and think about others? (Ironically, many conflicts do not arise out of ill-conceived intentions but mostly out of failure to be honest and straightforward with others, because we don't want to hurt their feelings.

The very definition of conflict is that perceptions we have of each other get fixed, stereotyped and distorted. Even the most caring and humane of us will easily ignore data that contradict the negative images we hold of a person and cling to only those observations that confirm our preconceptions. Of course, what makes it more complicated is the fact that our perceptions and opinions of people are not just based on figments of the imagination; they all have a grain of truth in them.

We could say that the purpose of this phase is twofold: (1) to re-align our soul forces of thinking, feelings, and intentions by means of perception sharing so that our interactions with people can become three-dimensional again. In other words, we learn to express what is truly living in us regarding our thoughts and feelings about a person. The truth is often less painful than a sugar-coated criticism or innuendo. (2) to gradually adjust our reality (self-perception) with the reality other people reflect back to us, thereby allowing the impact we have on others to be more consistent with our intentions.

4. Agreement and Contract Phase

If the conflict resolution resulted in the need to have certain forms of behavior and relationship change, then these changes must be clearly documented and agreed upon. For example, it may be that the parties agree to meet together on a weekly basis for the next three months in order to facilitate continued contact and communication. Or it may be agreed upon for the parties to journal their inner work on the issues surrounding the conflict and exchange these journals with each other periodically. Or it may be agreed upon to assign a "speaking partner" to each person. This colleague would function as an unbiased listener and advisor. There are numerous ways to accommodate further support and communication with the parties that are in conflict. All these agreements must be ratified and periodically reviewed. None of these arrangements should run forever. They are merely outer support systems that have a temporary value to assist people in making necessary behavioral changes.

5. Systems and Organization Development Phase

In some cases, part of resolving the conflict requires that changes be made in the structures and policies of the organization. It may be the formation of a new committee, or changes in membership, or amending certain procedures and policies. In extreme cases, it might even happen that the very foundation (vision or mission) of an organization is being challenged and is in need of re-vision. Individual development and organizational development is reciprocal: the one affects the other. As a rule, though, it would be a mistake to change the organizational structures before (or as a substitute for) working with the interpersonal conflict issues. Many organizations resort to making all kinds of system changes, only to find that these changes collapse because people cannot work together. The old maxim is still true: Systems are as good as the people who work in them.

6. Review and Implementation Phase

When any decision is made, we should be clear who, what, when, and how things are to be implemented. It is also important to maintain records outlining the conflict resolution process and results. Somewhere down the road there may be a need to refer back to the proceedings for administrative and/or legal purposes. At all times, maintain a record of the agreements and decisions, and read these back to the group before the meeting is adjourned.

The review process is the most important learning tool that we have at our disposal in group and organization development. In it we look back on our agreements and assess what worked well and what did not. Some of the guidelines regarding conflict resolution pertain to the review process as well. A properly conducted review neither judges nor intellectualizes. It merely describes and characterizes in images what transpired from an objective but real point of view. Do not fall into the trap of continuing your discussions and arguments. Make the review brief (7 minutes); just a couple of observations and descriptions will suffice. Stay with your personal learning and insights.

Leave others free to discover their own diamonds in the sand. Ask open-ended questions on what worked best and least. What would you have done differently? How did you personally contribute to the meeting? Where was the golden moment of opportunity? By means of the review process, organizations and people can engage in a continuous learning cycle and elevate even the most challenging experiences by finding meaning in them.

We have certainly entered a time of very dramatic changes in the political/social/economic conditions in the world. These changes are accompanied by the most severe conflicts. These conditions are a mirror of the difficulties we face in our own soul and spiritual development. We can expect these conflicts to intensify as time goes on. To the extent that we are successful in working with these challenges, we may not only serve our immediate communities but also contribute to a healthier society.

12

Group Exercises and Techniques

> If the group is an art form of the future, then convening groups is an artistry we must cultivate to fully harvest the promise of the future.
>
> *Centered on the Edge*
> —Jacob Needleman

Most of the following exercises are primarily part of a body of knowledge that was developed by The National Training Laboratory (NTL). The history of their organization can be found at http://www.ntl.org/about-history.html. This body of knowledge included group dynamics and development, group psychology, power and conflict, diversity awareness and training, leadership, and the concept of experiential learning. That, in turn, branched out into the field of organization development, and also outdoor challenge activities, such as Outward Bound, etc. Since then, numerous practitioners and organizations use their own variations by emphasizing different aspects of these exercises. All of the more familiar models—some copyrighted, some not—like Open Space and Appreciative Inquiry, trace most of their roots back to the National Training Laboratory.

Another great training organization with a rich tradition of T-group work that came out of the NTL was The Mid-Atlantic for Trainers and Consultants, Inc. (Geyer 1972).

The Fishbowl

The use of the fishbowl technique is a very powerful, profound, and efficient way to generate ideas, process information, or aid in resolving conflict. It gives the group a unique tool to objectively observe its inner workings and respond appropriately. The capacity to objectively observe is the first step to meaningful change. *In fact, in the very act of observing, the observed and observer cannot but change* (Anderson 1991). Sharing observations instead of expressing opinions is a fundamental communication skill.

The full group sits in a circle forming the fishbowl. A smaller group of 3–7 people—the fish—sits in a smaller circle in the center.

Rules:

1. An experienced facilitator must facilitate the exercise to set the ground rules, explain the exercise, monitor adherence to the conditions and intervene when necessary.
2. The inner circle is self-selected, never assigned. People can only volunteer after they are informed of the full process and intention of the exercise. This rule is to ensure that everyone is a willing and informed participant.
3. The issue or question at hand is assigned and agreed upon by all before volunteers are requested to sit in the smaller circle.
4. The first phase of the ensuing discussion should take no longer than about 20 minutes.
5. During the first phase of the conversation only the inner circle participants may speak. It is the aim that all members of the inner circle participate. The outer circle members never speak or intervene, except for the facilitator if necessary.
6. In the second phase, the people in the outer circle offer observations (not opinions or content comments) on what they witnessed, while the inner circle listens.

Process:

Each step is vital to the success of this exercise and cannot be skipped.

1. Explain the rules and conditions of the exercise. The entire exercise takes about 50–60 minutes.
2. Explore and agree on the topic to be discussed.
3. Ask for volunteers to sit in the inner circle.
4. The inner circle discusses the topic at hand for about 20 minutes.
5. The outer circle shares impressions and observations without coming to conclusions or judgments or adding to the substance of the topic discussed (10–15 minutes depending on the size of the group). Comments should be brief. Aim to have each observer make a contribution.
6. The inner circle is given a brief opportunity to relate the experience of working in the inner circle. Emotional content should be aired at least to the point that the participant can feel heard.
7. The inner and outer circles now join into one group again and continue with the agenda of the meeting.

There are several variations of this technique; it depends on the needs and circumstances. Here are some examples:

a. Instead of dividing the group into a smaller and larger group, the group can be divided in two equal parts. If this is done, steps 4, 5, and 6 are repeated for the outer circle as well. In this case, the process must be allotted twice the amount of time.

b. The group can be divided according to various criteria.

- It can be divided arbitrarily.
- It can be divided by gender.
- It can be divided by constituency: staff, executive, board, parents, volunteers, customers, etc.

c. In working with the biography or history of an institution, the smaller circle could be comprised of the founding members of the organization sharing their experiences and intentions of the early years.

d. Yet another application of this technique is to have a mandate group in the inner circle self-evaluating their work after completing their mandate. In this case, the technique is used as part of the overall evaluation process.

e. One, two, or three observers place themselves outside the full group. After the deliberations are complete, or at certain key points in the discussion, the observer(s) are placed in the center and share their observations on process, dynamics, how well the groups stayed on topic, the role of speaking and non-speaking members in the group. In other words, observations are shared on group process. This technique can be very helpful when the group has a hard time getting its work done, or when it is dealing with strong emotional content.

Giving and Receiving Feedback (Mirroring)

The intent of giving or receiving feedback is not to change someone's perceptions of self or of another, nor is it to drive home a point. The intent is to share perceptions in a respectful environment and in a respectful manner without any expectation of changing behavior or teaching lessons (Pfeiffer 1988). The intent is purely to exchange perceptions and leave the other completely free to accept (own) or reject the observations. This technique provides us the opportunity to hear how our actions and words come across to others and to bring these into line with our intentions.

The technique outlined below is rather formal. Time is set aside to go through this process carefully, usually in moments of inter-collegial difficulties. However, in the flow of a discussion a much shorter, informal version can be used to accommodate clearer communications.

Providing Feedback

- Seek permission from the intended recipient (honor a refusal).
- Address that person directly.
- Use "I" statements only. This means speaking from the first person. To use pronouns like, "we," or "they," or "one," throws a veil between the speaker and the listener.
- Never speak for others or from hearsay, but only from personal experience about how the recipient's comments or behavior affected you.
- Only use very specific, concrete and recent examples. It is best to use a recent example to which the others in the group bore witness.
- Do not editorialize, moralize, or philosophize; just describe.
- Make one statement at a time, after which the recipient paraphrases and asks questions for clarification, if needed.

Receiving Feedback

- Paraphrase feedback.
- Make sure you understand feedback or ask for clarification.

- Ask for examples and seek feedback from others to confirm or modify information.
- Do not accept generalities or hearsay.
- Never argue, defend your position, or give reasons. Let what is mirrored live in you. You are free to accept or reject the feedback in your mind.
- Be silent by listening carefully to the other.
- You are encouraged to solicit feedback from others.
- You may speak to how you were affected by the exchange: confused, helped, relieved, angered, supported, etc.
- You have the right to end the feedback at any time.

For All Members of the Circle

- Share new insights and what you have learned from the exchange.
- Remember that in the exchange, the value systems of both recipient and senders are operative; therefore do not judge.
- Each speaks from personal experience only.
- Avoid extreme responses.
- Repeat this process once or twice more, if needed.
- Never have one person continuously sit in the "hot seat," but move the process on to other members of the group.
- If given in a helpful way, feedback can be a wonderful gift for both the recipient and the sender. Look upon it as a great opportunity for recipients and the group.

Brainstorming Technique

The purpose of this technique (Phillips 1989) is to generate ideas in an unencumbered, free-flowing, non-critical fashion. It allows smaller groups to "think outside the box," and come up with creative solutions.

> Notes:
> As much as possible, all members are responsible for the process. If the process is compromised, any member can call time-out to check with the group and bring the discussion and process back on track.
>
> This process will appear quite regimented and difficult, at first. However, it is very important that each step is applied. After practice, you will find that the results are effective, efficient and have a higher quality of interaction.

Process:

1. All members of the group place themselves in a circle (making eye contact). There is no note taking. There are no objects (tables, books, etc.) between participants. A blank flip chart is placed outside the circle for notation of final decision or proposal. One of the group members functions as a timekeeper. The group determines the length of the meeting beforehand.
2. The question or issue and desirable outcome are briefly described and written up. Everyone must be clear on the task at hand before proceeding to the next step.
3. In a creative brainstorming session of about 15 minutes, possible options/solutions/ideas are

explored. There is no discussion at this point on any item contributed. Only questions for clarification. Everyone participates. The more out-of-the-box thinking, the better. The pace of discussion should be fast and energizing.

4. Members of the group take a brief personal time to think silently to review the contributions on the flipchart and prioritize the items. No further items are solicited. Then the group compares notes and selects the 2 or 3 top items receiving the most votes.
5. A 20–30 minute discussion on each discussion item. One or two points per person at a time. The objective is that all group members get to speak. If possible, each speaker briefly paraphrases the main point of the previous speaker before adding his/her contribution. The point is to add to each other's comments in an attempt to build a common picture.
6. If any member of the group senses that an agreement might be close, he/she may articulate a proposal or summation of the agreement by writing it down on the flip chart. The group discussion continues for about 15 to 20 minutes. The final decision could be agreed either by consensus or by majority vote.

Exercises in Working with Conflict

What follow are a few exercises for use in conflict resolution. In each exercise, any number of variations is possible. Be creative!

- Have opposing parties, in twos, sit across from each other and draw a self-portrait. When finished, they exchange pictures and each describes the picture of the other. Then, for 10 minutes, both articulate what new insights they gained about the other through this experience.

- Have all parties draw, paint or model an image of the conflict. Then, a general discussion is conducted about the nature of the conflict.

- Have each participant silently conduct an imaginary conversation with a person with whom he or she has a real conflict. The conversation should include a confrontation—what the other says and what you would say and do in response. After 15 minutes, the participant writes down the essence of the conversation and may share this with the full group. The participant should identify helpful behavior and what was most difficult about the exercise. As an option, the full group could offer helpful feedback.

- One exercise in trust building starts with half of the group blindfolded. The sighted people each take a person without sight, and guide this person through the building or out through the garden/park/street. The sighted person gives full account of all the obstacles on the way. Next, roles should be reversed. Afterwards, the group shares insights and experiences.

- Biography exercises are mandatory for promoting trust. As a guideline, avoid long accounts of a person's life and history. Design specific questions to which people one by one briefly respond. Examples:
    a. Describe your favorite room or place when you were a young child.
    b. What is your very first memory?

c. Describe the first time that you truly felt independent (the world is my oyster).
d. What spoken or unspoken rule lived in your family during your teens?
e. What was your favorite toy, and why?
f. How did you first experience leadership in yourself or another?

Then, from the answers received, draw parallels to and contrasts with the present situation. From these insights, we may also extrapolate future intentions or resolutions.

Epilogue

One of the most vexing and existential questions facing organizations is how they can change when change is needed. Some of the changes take place because of external conditions and circumstances. That includes transitioning from one phase into the next. But can change happen when people seek it even against prevailing unhelpful patterns? The answer is yes, but—only with extraordinary effort and dedication.

Which brings us to the role of the external consultant (Block 2000). This role could be divided into two categories: One is the consultant with specific technical expertise in operational systems. Operational systems like accounting, computer networking and software, production, finance, acquisition, marketing, and so forth—or, in the case of an educational institution, curriculum development. The other branch is a people-centered consultancy. This branch deals with communication, personnel, collegiality, organizational culture, differences and conflict, and overall organizational development; in other words, the "soft side" of an institution.

These two branches naturally overlap in many areas. *There is a consensus, however, that the so-called soft side is the hardest to manage and change.* In the second area of endeavor, purposeful change can never be driven from the outside of the organization. In this case, the consultant's role is purely one of facilitating rather than problem solving. The moment a consultant gives advice, he or she splits the organization between those who heed the advice and those who oppose it. Even in the rare instance when advice is universally accepted, and/or fully embraced by the leadership, its long-term positive effect is minimal. Yet, when people are in deep disagreement or at a loss for a workable solution, they will plead for someone to tell them what to do. The experienced consultant will resist the temptation to free a work community from its dilemma.

To rescue a community from its predicament only postpones the day of reckoning when an organization must go through the eye of the needle to find new ways of working. *An experienced external facilitator can create and hold a space in which all members of an institution can do their work.* This role is not unlike the function a belay rope fills in the art of rock climbing. The rope is there as a safety device. It gives the climber the confidence to conquer greater heights, and in case of a misstep, the ability to regain her footing and resume the climb on her own. That's the true and only correct role of the external change agent in organizational development.

Lasting cultural change (how we do things, and how we relate to each other) comes about from within the membership of an organization. System changes can come from outside expertise, but even these recommendations would have to be re-visited from time to time in order to stay current.

I hope this book provides all of the methodologies and tools necessary for meaningful change. It rests upon the shoulders of each and every member of an organization to imbue these guidelines with life.

Bibliography

Andersen, Tom. (ed) (1991) *The Reflecting Team: Dialogues and Dialogues About the Dialogues*. New York, NY: W.W. Norton and Company.

Block, Peter. "The End of Leadership," *Leader to Leader*, Number 3, Winter 1997. Drucker Foundation and Jossey-Bass, Inc.

———. "Finding Community at Work," *Journal for Quality and Participation*. September, 1994.

———. (2000) *Flawless Consulting Fieldbook and Companion: A Guide to Understanding Your Expertise*. San Francisco, CA: Jossey Bass.

Bohm, David. (1991) *Wholeness and the Implicate Order*. London, UK: Ark Paperback.

Briggs, John and David F. Peat. (1971) *Turbulent Mirror*. New York, NY: Harper and Row, Publishers, Inc.

Casti, John L. (2000) *Five more Golden Rules: Knots, Codes, Chaos and other Great Theories of 20th Century Mathematics*. New York, NY: John Wiley and Sons, Inc.

Conforti, Michael. (1999) *Field, Form and Fate: Patterns in Mind, Nature and Psyche*. Woodstock, CT: Spring Publications, Inc.

Denham, John, ed. "Conflict and Power Utilization." Human Relationship Reader. Mid-Atlantic Association for Training and Consulting, Inc. 1978.

De Pree, Max. (1992) *Leadership Jazz*. New York, NY: Bantam Doubleday Dell Publishing Group, Inc.

Emery, Fred E. and Eric L. Trist. (1973) *Toward a Social Ecology*. New York, NY: Plenum.

Emery, Merrelyn, ed. (Revised 1993) *Participative Design for Participative Democracy*. Centre for Continuing Education. Canberra, Australia: Australian University.

Emery, Merrelyn and Ronald E. Purser. (1996) *The Search Conference: A Powerful Method for Planning Organizational Change and Community Action*. San Francisco, CA: Jossey-Bass, Inc.

Estes, Caroline. "Consensus Ingredients" *Context: A Quarterly Journal of Humane Sustainable Culture* Fall 1983.

Forbess-Greene, Sue. (1989) *The Encyclopedia of Icebreakers*. San Diego, CA: University Associates. Inc.

Geyer, Nancy B. "Designing Structured Experiential Learning." Basic Reader in Human Relationship Training. Mid-Atlantic Association for Training and Consulting, Inc. Washington, DC. 1972.

———. "Problem Solving, Goal Setting and Decision Making." Basic Reader in Human Relationship Training. Mid-Atlantic Association of Training and Consulting, Inc. Washington, DC. 1972.

Gleick, James. (1987) *Chaos: Making a New Science*. New York, NY: Penguin Books, USA, Inc.

Goethe, Johann Wolfgang von. (1999) *The Green Snake and the Beautiful Lily*. Stroud, UK: Hawthorn Press.

Harrison, Roger (1983) "Strategies for a New Age," *Human Resource Management*, Vol. 22, No. 3, pp. 209-325.

Langs, Robert, MD. (1993) *Unconscious Communication in Everyday Life*. Northvale, NJ: Jason Aronson, Inc.

Laszlo, Ervin. (1993) *The Creative Cosmos: A Unification Science of Matter, Life and Mind*. Edinburgh, Scotland: Floris Books.

Lewin, Roger. (1992) *Complexity: Life at the Edge of Chaos*. Chicago, IL: The University of Chicago Press.

Lievegoed, Bernard J. C. (1973) *The Developing Organization: Organizations, People, and Society*. (Tr. J. Collins) London, UK: Travistock.

———. (1979) *Phases*. London, UK: Rudolf Steiner Press.

———. (1992) *The Battle of the Soul*. London, UK: Rudolf Steiner Press.

Loye, David. (1983) *An Arrow Through Chaos: How We See into the Future*. Rochester, NY: Park Street Press.

Mitchell, David, (ed.) (1999) *Administrative Explorations*. Boulder, CO: The Economic/Legal Committee, AWSNA.

———. (1992) *The Art of Waldorf School Administration*. Boulder, CO: The Economic/Legal Committee, AWSNA.

Morley, Barry. (1993) *Beyond Consensus: Salvaging Sense of The Meeting*. Philadelphia, PA: Pendle Hill.

Napier, Augustus Y., Ph.D. and Carl Whitaker, M.D. (1988) . *The Family Crucible: The Intense Experience of Family Therapy*. New York, NY: Harper and Row.

Needleman, Jacob. (2003) *A Sense of the Cosmos: The Encounter of Modern Science and Ancient Truth*. Rhinebeck, NY: Monkfish Book Publishing.

Pfeiffer, J. William and John E. Jones. (1988) *A Handbook of Structured Experiences for Human Relations Training*. San Diego, CA: University Associates, Inc.

Phillips, Steven L. and Robin L. Elledge. (1989) *The Team Building Resource Book*. San Diego, CA: University Associates, Inc.

Pieterse, Cornelis. "Mandate Systems" and "Principles of Communication and their Practical Application." *Administrative Explorations*. Boulder, CO. The Economic/Legal Committee, AWSNA, David Mitchell, ed., 1999.

———. "Working Together: A Guide to Conflict Resolution." *The Art of Waldorf School Administration*. Boulder, CO. The Economic/Legal Committee, AWSNA, David Mitchell, ed., 1992.

Rappaport, Julian. "In Praise of Paradox: A Social Policy of Empowerment of Prevention." *American Journal of Community Psychology*. Vol. 9, Number 1, February 1981.

Rosenfeld, Albert and Lennart Nilsson. "Drama of Life before Birth." *Life*. April 30th, 1965.

Senge, Peter M. (1990) *The Fifth Discipline: The Art and Practice of the Learning Organization*. New York, NY: Bantam Doubleday Dell Publishing Group. Inc.

Steiner, Rudolf. (1974) *Awakening to Community*. Spring Valley, NY: Anthroposophic Press, Inc.

———. *Wahrspruchworte* (GA 40).

Thibault, J.W. (1959) *The Social Psychology of Groups*. New York, NY: John Wiley.

Thoreau, Henry. (1995) *Walden: or Life in the Woods*. New York, NY: Dover Publications, Inc.

Trist, E.L. and F.E. Emery. (1960) Report on the Barford Course for Bristol/Siddeley, July 10–16, 1960. Travistock Document No. 598, London, September.

Wachsmuth, Guenther. (1955) *The Life and Work of Rudolf Steiner.* Trans. Reginald Raab and Olin Wannamaker. New York: Whittier Books, Inc.

Wheatley, Margaret. (1992) *Leadership and the New Sciences: Learning about Organization from an Orderly Universe*. San Francisco, CA: Berrett-Koehler Publishers, Inc.

Weisbord, Marvin R. (1992) *Discovering Common Ground: How Future Search Conferences Bring People Together to Achieve Breakthrough Innovation, Empowerment, Shared Vision, and Collaborative Action*. San Francisco, CA: Berrett-Koehler, Publishers, Inc. http://www.futuresearch.net/

Weisbord , Marvin R. and Sandra Janoff. (2000, 1995) 2nd ed. *Future Search: An Action Guide to Finding Common Ground in Organizations and Communities*. San Francisco, CA: Berrett-Koehler Publishers, Inc.

Yalom, Irvin D. (1985) *The Theory and Practice of Group Psychotherapy*. New York, NY: Basic Books, A Division of Harper Collins Publishers.

Cornelis Pieterse is senior partner and owner of Lemnis Associates in Wilton, New Hampshire. He has been consulting and facilitating with numerous Waldorf Schools, small businesses, civic organizations and corporations since the late 1980s. He specializes in the arts of decision making, consensus building, visioning and planning for diverse and often conflicted communities, team building, coaching and leading facilitation workshops.

Together with his wife and three other couples, he was a co-founder of the Chicago Waldorf School (1972) and of The Lukas Foundation in Temple, NH (1980), a group home for adults with developmental disabilities. He was the board chair of this foundation for 11 years.

With six of his friends and colleagues, he is part of the coordinating group for the Lemnis Conference Series based in the Northwest. For twelve years, these conferences provided a forum for teachers, administrators, board members and volunteers to meet and share best practices, to network, to study, to create art, and to experience the essentials of community building through the art of conversation.

Cornelis received his Waldorf teacher training from Emerson College, UK (1969), a Bachelor of Arts in Philosophy from Loyola University of Chicago, and his Master of Arts in Marriage and Family Therapy from Antioch New England Graduate School, Keene, New Hampshire.

Cornelis lives with his wife Mickey in Wilton. He has three wonderful sons—Donavan, Shawn and Joshua—each a Waldorf school alumnus and accomplished in his chosen field of endeavor.

He can be contacted at:

Lemnis Associates
227 Temple Road, Wilton, NH 03086
603-654-2116
Cornelis@Lemnis.com
www.Lemnis.com